D1359301

Especially For

_____

From

_____

Date

_____

Circle of Friends

Shared Blessings

Inspiration for a Woman's Soul

BARBOUR
PUBLISHING

Circle of Friends is a ministry of women helping women. Born out of a small account-ability group which led to a women's Bible study, Circle of Friends Ministries is now a nonprofit organization dedicated to encouraging women to find and follow Christ. Our desire is to encourage one another to love God more deeply and to follow Him with a heart of passion that reaches out and draws others along with us on our journey.

"Circle of Friends are women of biblical depth and compassion for others. They have a knack for bringing humor, hope, and practical application to everyday situations."

—Carol Kent, Speaker and Author
When I Lay My Isaac Down and
A New Kind of Normal

"Circle of Friends has its finger on the pulse of the heart-needs of women today. Through word and song they link arms with women around the globe to bring the hope and healing of Jesus Christ."

—Sharon Jaynes, Speaker and Author
Becoming a Woman Who Listens to God and
Extraordinary Moments with God

Introduction

Who can understand the heart of a woman—with all its joys and triumphs, challenges and heartaches—better than another woman? We are told in Titus that mature women of the faith are to be "teachers of good things," and in Hebrews that we are to "exhort (encourage) one another daily."

Shared Blessings is a devotional written by women who have a passion and love for Jesus. Their stories, insights, biblical applications, and their refreshing honesty in everyday trials in their lives will encourage your heart and strengthen your faith. So grab a cup of coffee or tea, pull up a chair and share life, share blessings, with your "Circle of Friends." You'll laugh, you'll cry, you'll find that you truly have found a place to belong. . . .

A Blessed Life

"For I know the plans I have for you," declares the LORD, "plans to prosper you and not to harm you, plans to give you hope and a future."

JEREMIAH 29:11 NIV

How secure would you be if you knew your life had a plan no one could thwart? Would you step forward with confidence and hope? Would it mean the difference between mediocrity and the best in your life?

God has just such a well-planned future for the believer who trusts in Him. He pointed out His plan for the nation of Judah, when it was completely disobedient to Him. The people were not going in the right direction, and God had so much more for them, if they would give up their wicked ways and walk into the blessings He had in mind for them.

Sin never offers the benefits of God's plan. At best it offers quick thrills, followed by long-standing regrets. Its eternal plan is miserable: an eternity separated from God, filled with suffering. Compare that to the blessings of a life on this earth that serves God and an eternity of joy in His presence.

Don't settle for Satan's second-best plan. God has a plan for you!

Pamela McQuade
Daily Wisdom for the Workplace

God Is Enough!

Not that we are sufficient of ourselves to think any thing as of ourselves; but our sufficiency is of God.

2 Corinthians 3:5 kjv

God's presence is literally and truly all we need for everything.

Every fear, every perplexity, every anxiety find an all-satisfying answer in God—what He is in nature and character. He can only act according to His character, and therefore what is His character is the one vital thing we need to know. If He is good, unselfish, loving, wise, and just and, with all this, omnipotent and omnipresent as well, then all must be ordered right for us. It cannot be otherwise.

The seen things may seem to be all wrong, but we know that the seen thing is very often not at all the true thing. What we are able to see is generally only a partial view, and no partial view can be depended on. One must have, what George MacDonald calls "eyes that can see below surfaces," if one is to do justice to a good God. But when His utter unselfishness has been discovered, this interior eye is opened, and all difficulties as to the apparent mysteries of His dealings are answered forever.

It may not seem to our consciousness that any prayers are answered or any promises fulfilled, but what of that? Behind every prayer and behind every promise, there is God; and if He exists at all, we know He must be enough.

Nothing else really matters—neither creeds nor ceremonies nor doctrines nor dogmas. God is; God is unselfish; and God is enough!

Hannah Whitall Smith
The Unselfishness of God

A Child of the Father

How great is the love the Father has lavished on us,
that we should be called children of God!
And that is what we are!

1 JOHN 3:1 NIV

It is not hard for the Lord to lead, and, therefore, asking God for guidance gives you a wonderful opportunity for hidden companionship with Him. It is such a comfort to know that before we were born, God had already made His plan for us. He gave us gifts and qualities, and He will surely not waste them now that you are a Christian! He, our good Shepherd, knows your physical, emotional, and spiritual needs better than you do. He said, "I will never leave you nor forsake you" (Joshua 1:5 NIV). He knows the end from the beginning and can allow all that you do and experience work for the good of yourself and others, if only we could better understand what it means to be a child of God.

When you accept God as your Savior, He, your Redeemer and Lord, makes you a child of God. If you have not done that yet, I hope that you accept Him now. But we have to understand what it means to be a child of God. God is our Father, who loves us. We are a part of Him. It is not hard work for Him to lead us; He thinks it's wonderful, and there is nothing too great for His omnipotence and nothing too small for His love.

Corrie ten Boom
Reflections of God's Glory

Blessed Security

You have wearied the Lord with your words.
"How have we wearied him?" you ask. You have
wearied him by saying that all who do evil are good
in the Lord's sight, and he is pleased with them.
You have wearied him by asking,
"Where is the God of justice?"

The attitude behind these ostensibly innocuous words is: "This isn't fair; we deserve better than this!" When's the last time your man left or your dog died. . .or something even worse happened and you told God you deserved better?

There's a huge difference between understanding God's love for us, and the sense of entitlement displayed by Malachi's peers at the end of chapter 2. When our security rests in God's love for us, it is manifest in humility, gratitude, and love for others. We become God—and others—centered. But entitlement will always manifest itself in an arrogant demand to have our needs and wants met. Entitlement is self-centered.

It's critical for us to learn that the opposite of arrogance is not insecurity; frankly insecurity and arrogance are fruit from the same tree. Christians who wear their feelings on their sleeve, are quick to take offense, and reek of anxiety are not humble; they're big fat babies! The opposite of arrogance is security. It's the deep-seated confidence that God holds us in the palm of His hand and nothing can separate us from His love. That kind of security is what gives us the ability to focus on God instead of ourselves.

Lisa Harper
Tough Love, Tender Mercies

Perfect People Need Not Apply

But Moses said to God, "Who am I, that I should go to Pharaoh and bring the Israelites out of Egypt?"

EXODUS 3:11 NIV

I recently read a bumper sticker that said, GOD DOESN'T CALL THE QUALIFIED; HE QUALIFIES THE CALLED.

In a world that demands qualifications for just about everything, isn't it nice that God demands only our willingness to serve Him? In fact, God calls imperfect people.

Besides that, Moses had a speech problem—yet God was asking him to approach Pharaoh and tell him to let God's people go free. Moses knew he wasn't qualified. In fact, he said to God, "O Lord, I have never been eloquent, neither in the past nor since you have spoken to your servant. I am slow of speech and tongue" (Exodus 4:10 NIV).

But the Lord already knew that, and He still wanted Moses for the job. He said to Moses, "Who gave man his mouth? Who makes him deaf or mute? Who gives him sight or makes him blind? Is it not I, the Lord? Now go; I will help you speak and will teach you what to say" (Exodus 4:11–12 NIV).

God knows all of your shortcomings—and He doesn't care. He just wants your willing heart and availability.

Michelle Medlock Adams
Secrets of Happiness

Resting in His Love

*I am convinced that neither death nor life, neither
angels nor demons, neither the present nor the future,
nor any powers, neither height nor depth, nor anything
else in all creation, will be able to separate us from the
love of God that is in Christ Jesus our Lord.*

ROMANS 8:38–39 NIV

Get up early. Get the kids off to school. Go
to work. Walk in the door and fix dinner. Help
the kids with homework and then run them to
football practice. Come home, fold laundry, do
the dishes. Go get the kids at football practice.
Motivate them to get showers, fix them more
food, attempt to have devotions with them, kisses
good night, answer their last fifty questions before
they sleep, and then fall into bed. Get up early and
do it again. That doesn't even include cleaning.
You mean we are supposed to clean?

Women balancing life. Some days we think we can do this thing well, and we strive to stay on top of every detail. But the days we are running behind or nothing is going right, we can become discouraged. We may wonder what our purpose is or if anything beneficial is being accomplished. The Word of God says that nothing can separate us from the love of God. As women we try to accomplish much—sometimes too much. God reminds us that we don't need to strive so hard. We can rest in His love. No matter what struggles we face, His love is greater. We have found a place to belong.

Jocelyn Hamsher
Circle of Friends

Blessed Freedom

Godly sorrow brings repentance that leads to salvation and leaves no regret, but worldly sorrow brings death.

2 Corinthians 7:10 niv

If we are feeling condemnation, it is not coming from God. Satan condemns. The Holy Spirit convicts. How do we know the difference? Satan accuses us to make us feel condemned. The Holy Spirit convicts us to bring us to repentance (2 Corinthians 7:9–10). Once we have repented and asked for forgiveness, it is finished, over and done with, wiped away. If feelings of condemnation persist, they are a result of listening to the accusations of the enemy. . .listening to the lie. . . .

The feeling of not being able to forgive myself is steeped in self-loathing—anger with myself or blaming myself. Satan tries to keep us in a morbid mindset of self-loathing. It is part of his job description as "accuser of the brethren." It comes in the form of "you deserve what you got." "You made your bed, now lie in it." Not only that, "You made your bed, now you stay in it."

Satan knows that the slightest whisper of guilt is easily received by a fragile heart plundered by life. Do not let the enemy convince you to stay in the prison of guilt and shame. The sentence has already been served. You are free to go.

Sharon Jaynes
"I'm Not Good Enough". . .
and Other Lies Women Tell Themselves

The Blessing of a Renewed Mind

Be transformed by the renewing of your mind.

ROMANS 12:2 NIV

Emotions are a normal part of life. As human beings, each of us has a full range of emotions—love, happiness, joy, delight, peace, disappointment, loss, grief, doubt, compassion, sadness, depression, jealousy, anger, bitterness, guilt, and many others.

Throughout the Bible, women and men—even Jesus—display a variety of emotions. I imagine that Adam and Eve were deliriously happy in the Garden of Eden. The woman caught in adultery and pushed before a condemning crowd must have felt humiliation. Mary, the virgin mother of Jesus, was fearful when she learned she was pregnant, then joyful when she discovered the news was true— she would give birth to the Savior of the world! David was afraid for his life while Saul pursued him with murderous intent. And Jesus felt alone, broken to the point of sweating blood, as He prayed for His life to be spared.

Emotions can be powerful—even overwhelming at times. When our emotions aren't processed in healthy ways, they can get stuck like a clogged drain. Help comes when we surrender our feelings to the One who has the power to blast away our emotional congestion.

Prayer is essential to managing emotions. In fact, it transforms us. To change how we feel, we need to adjust the way we think. When we alter the way we view our situations, we can change the way we respond to them—with wisdom, rather than impulsive actions we may regret later.

With God's help, we can get through both the valleys and the victories of life.

Jackie M. Johnson
Power Prayers for Women

Forwarding Grace

Shouldest not thou also have had compassion on thy fellowservant, even as I had pity on thee?

MATTHEW 18:33 KJV

*I*f you've ever worked for a compassionate boss when your life was filled with stress, you recognize what a blessing this attribute is. If your boss gave you sympathy, support, and encouragement while you faced challenges at home or in the workplace, you've been blessed with a wonderful person to work for.

But compassion is not wimpiness. Supporting a person through a trial doesn't equate with a lack of accountability, as the man in this parable learned. He'd been in debt, and his master forgave what he owed. In turn, the greedy servant tried to extract every penny from other servants who owed him some cash. When his master found out about it, he was extremely angry that the servant had not passed on a similar mercy.

We need to have compassion and respect it when it's given to us. For a time, we receive an unusual grace, but we cannot take advantage. That would be like taking for granted the mercy God has given us in saving us—which is what this parable is about, after all. God gave us His grace, and we are simply to pass it on in all things.

Pamela McQuade
Daily Wisdom for the Workplace

Freedom in Christ

*Lord, who may dwell in your sanctuary? Who may
live on your holy hill? He whose walk is blameless
and who does what is righteous, who speaks the
truth from his heart.*

PSALM 15:1–2 NIV

When Jesus was addressing a group of Jews
who had professed a level of belief in Him, He
said to them, "You shall know the truth, and the
truth shall make you free" (John 8:32 NKJV).

Free from what? they asked. They didn't understand what Jesus was talking about. They protested
that they had never been slaves, conveniently
ignoring their present position being ruled over
by a Roman government. Jesus was not talking,
however, about political freedom. He was talking
about freedom from sin, from fear, from the dark

cellars of our lives, freedom from the dictates of our inner events.

Part of my healing was facing everything that was true about my life: why I behaved the way I did when I felt unloved, where the barely repressed anger came from, how I used sarcasm as a shield around my soul, why I felt so alone even in a crowd of friends. In facing these ugly parts of my soul I was able to bring them into the light of God's grace. I saw that I couldn't be free if I wouldn't face what was true.

The freedom that Christ offers is the fruit of facing the truth, no matter how ugly it is or how ashamed we feel.

Sheila Walsh
The Heartache No One Sees

Blessed Simplicity

Not that I speak in respect of want: for I have learned, in whatsoever state I am, therewith to be content.

The last time my husband and I stayed with our Amish friends in Pennsylvania, I observed their grandchildren playing together. They weren't bored and didn't complain because there was nothing to do. They found enjoyment in simple things like reading, playing a ball game, petting their dog, riding their scooters, swinging, and swimming in the pond. They didn't need computers or electronic games. They laughed and talked together and didn't send text messages in order to communicate.

In our fast-paced electronic age

many "Englishers" don't take the time to enjoy the simple things life has to offer. We rush from place to place, hurry to complete our tasks, and find that our lives are full of stress and worry. We've become exhausted and discontented because we don't spend enough quality time with our family and friends. Many people strive so hard to get ahead that they don't see what's right beside them. Material things don't bring true happiness, nor do they bring lasting contentment. When we look around at the beauty God created, and find joy in being with those we love, our discontent fades and appreciation sets in.

Wanda E. Brunstetter
A Celebration of the Simple Life

Daily Bread

You shall walk after the LORD your God and fear Him, and keep His commandments and obey His voice; you shall serve Him and hold fast to Him.

DEUTERONOMY 13:4 NKJV

When I don't want to hear God's voice, I get busy with important things, "spiritual things" that everyone knows take a lot of time. Before long an uncomfortable feeling sets in, gentle but urgent, like a mouse nibbling at my toes. I can't stand it until things are right again with God and me. . . .

To hear God's voice, I must want to. I mean *want to*. It's not optional, like breakfast. I also need a listening place where I'm quiet and alone enough to hear Him. When we live on every word that comes from His mouth that means eating up God's Word like the daily Bread it is. And why wouldn't we? It's fresh baked daily just for us. Open your Bible and Jesus brings the meal!

Our family doctor admits he has a little weight problem. But then, who wouldn't when his family owns the largest Italian bakery in the area? Every morning before dawn a delivery truck brings him fresh hot bread and Italian rolls right to his front door. He wouldn't think of not eating them. Neither would I. Imagine smelling the aroma waiting for you every day in God's Word. Fresh words just for you. Rise and eat, child. You look hungry.

Virelle Kidder
Meet Me at the Well

Overcoming Fear

There is no fear in love; but perfect love casts out fear, because fear involves torment. But he who fears has not been made perfect in love.

1 JOHN 4:18 NKJV

Identifying our fears and admitting we have a problem is only the beginning. Most of us have struggled for a lifetime with fear at some level. I've been frustrated by an underlying belief that "godly Christian women" aren't supposed to struggle with phobias, fears, and anxieties, because "trusting the Lord" should be more than enough to handle any problem. So I'm a failure. Now what?

The first step to finding a solution is to acknowledge that there are times when we question our faith and struggle with fear. Some of us have had fleeting thoughts of suicide. Most often, instead of physical suicide, we experience emotional suicide. Fear becomes "comfortable" because it's familiar. We're used to feeling like powerless victims in the fear monster's kingdom. Instead of taming the monster and enjoying our lives, we allow ourselves to die slowly by many of the following prescriptions: denial, addictions, withdrawal, control, shame, and self-hatred.

Overcoming lifelong fear is inconvenient. The process destroys carefully constructed facades. It leaves one feeling naked. Unprotected. Vulnerable. Exposed. It seems odd to speak of fear as "safe," but as with any long-term companion— even a cruel one—saying good-bye is difficult.

Facing our fear head-on can feel intensely risky. But it can be a stepping-stone to humble faith, renewed confidence, appropriate power and courage, and trusting reverence toward a sovereign, powerful, and loving God.

Carol Kent
Tame Your Fears

A Blessed Example

*That they may teach the young women to be sober,
to love their husbands, to love their children, to be
discreet, chaste, keepers at home, good, obedient
to their own husbands, that the word of God be
not blasphemed.*

TITUS 2:4–5 KJV

My grandmother was a woman of exemplary piety, and from her I learned many useful and abiding lessons. She was a firm believer in prayer and, when I was very young, taught me to believe that our Father in heaven will always give us whatever is for our good; and therefore that we should be careful not to ask Him anything that is not consistent with His holy will.

At evening time she used to call me to her dear old rocking chair; then we would kneel down together and repeat some simple petition. Many years afterward when my grandmother had departed from earth and the rocking chair had passed into other hands, in grateful memory, I wrote a poem entitled, "Grandma's Rocking Chair":

There are forms that flit before me,
There are tones I yet recall;
But the voice of gentle Grandma
I remember best of all.

In her loving arms she held me,
And beneath her patient care
I was borne away to dreamland
In her dear old rocking chair.

Fanny Crosby
Memories of Eighty Years

God as Husband

He has taken me to the banquet hall,
and his banner over me is love.

SONG OF SOLOMON 2:4 NIV

Everyone on the face of the earth longs to be loved and to give love. God made us that way on purpose, hoping that we would turn to Him and revel in the fullness of His love. But He realized that we needed something that showed us what intimacy should feel like, so He created human relationships as the example. These relationships, however, were never designed to replace the love relationship we were created to have with Him.

Whether you're single or not, my question to you is this: Who are you married to—God or the world? The world is a difficult husband. It is demanding, ungracious, and selfish. And life with someone who doesn't love you back is hard.

God, however, is a loving partner, pouring out countless benefits and lavishing us with constant reminders of His care for us. So how do we get in on all those wonderful blessings? How do we get back on the road to loving Him according to His original design? How do we leave the labor of being a Christian behind and get back to the good life? It's actually easier than you think. If you're up to the challenge, I dare you to get a love life with God.

Michelle McKinney Hammond
A Sassy Girl's Guide to Loving God

Blessed Joy

*But may the righteous be glad and rejoice before
God; may they be happy and joyful.*

Psalm 68:3 NIV

*W*here does joy come from?

True joy is not fleeting nor dependent on our circumstances. Though the world may seem intent on squelching our happiness, we can learn to pray powerfully for more joy in our lives. It starts with asking.

"This is the confidence we have in approaching God," the apostle John wrote in 1 John 5:14–15 (NIV), "that if we ask anything according to his will, he hears us. And if we know that he hears us—whatever we ask—we know that we have what we asked of him."

Of course, the timing is God's prerogative. A

woman named Sarah knew that God answers prayer, but she wasn't willing to wait on Him. She wanted a son, and in spite of God's promise to her husband, Abraham, she tried to arrange for the baby's birth by a surrogate, her servant Hagar. Hagar's son, Ishmael, caused much grief to Sarah—but God was gracious and ultimately provided Sarah and Abraham the son, Isaac, He had promised long before.

In surrendering our will for God's and following His commands, we can realize more of His power and joy in our lives. A heart full of joy is a heart that sings praise and thanks to God. Praising Him multiplies our joy and increases our faith.

Praising and thanking God—for who He is and all He has done—will make any hard day better.

Jackie M. Johnson
Power Prayers for Women

Turned Inside Out

Bless the LORD, O my soul; and all that is within me, bless His holy name! Bless the LORD, O my soul, and forget not all His benefits.

PSALM 103:1–2 NKJV

Have you turned your life inside out before God? My purse is a catchall. After a while it gets stuffed to the point I literally have to turn it upside down and inside out to sort through all the junk. Along with the bits and pieces of paper and trash are those unexpected items I put in there to take care of later. All of it accumulates until I get down to business and clean it out.

Our spiritual lives can be like that. If we are to bless the Lord with all that is within us we first must get rid of the "junk"—that is, anything that is keeping us from a whole and complete relationship with God. What's in your spiritual purse? A bad attitude, selfishness, worry, doubt, lack of faith?

Too often we can try to hide areas of our lives and, like my purse, this only works for so long before we can't hold any more "stuff." When we are transparent before God and others, it keeps us clean, confessing our sin and moving us forward. Then we can, along with the psalmist, bless the Lord with everything we have and offer our gratitude and praise without barriers or hindrance.

Missy Horsfall
Circle of Friends

The Adorable Will of Our God

And he made known to us the mystery of his will according to his good pleasure, which he purposed in Christ.

Ephesians 1:9 NIV

A great many Christians actually seem to think that all their Father in heaven wants is a chance to make them miserable, and to take away all their blessings, and they imagine, poor souls, that if they hold on to things in their own will, they can hinder Him from doing this. I am ashamed to write the words, and yet we must face a fact which is making wretched hundreds of lives.

Better and sweeter than health or friends or money or fame or ease or prosperity is the adorable will of our God. It gilds the darkest hours with a divine halo and sheds brightest sunshine on the gloomiest paths. He always reigns who has made it His kingdom; and nothing can go amiss to Him.

Surely, then, it is nothing but a glorious privilege that is opening before you when I tell you that the first step you must take in order to enter into the life hid with Christ in God, is that of entire consecration. I cannot have you look at it as a hard and stern demand. You must do it gladly, thankfully, enthusiastically. You must go in on what I call the privilege side of consecration; and I can assure you, from a blessed experience, that you will find it the happiest place you have ever entered yet.

Hannah Whitall Smith
The Christian's Secret of a Happy Life

Blessed Nobility

A wife of noble character who can find? She is worth far more than rubies. Her husband has full confidence in her and lacks nothing of value.

PROVERBS 31:10–11 NIV

Today, more than ever before, a woman of noble character is hard to find. To be noble means to be dignified and gracious. In the Amplified Bible, the word for noble is rendered "capable, intelligent, and virtuous." A woman like that is not easy to come by anymore.

God wants us to stand out as women who know we have something valuable to offer the world. We are capable, intelligent, and virtuous women who inspire full confidence in those who rely on us most, whether our husband, children, employer, or co-workers. The people around us can have full confidence in us because we have full confidence in God and we live accordingly.

You can have full confidence in God no matter what season of life you're in right now. Maybe you're a mother at home with small children. Or an empty nester. You may be single. . .or single again. I don't know what situation you're in, but I do know who is in the midst of that situation with you: a loving God who cares so much for you that He paid the ultimate price so you and He never have to spend even one day apart.

Donna Partow
Becoming the Woman God Wants Me to Be

Belonging to God

"Ho! Everyone who thirsts, come to the waters; and you who have no money, come, buy and eat. Yes, come, buy wine and milk without money and without price."

ISAIAH 55:1 NKJV

Have you wandered away from God? Perhaps following Him just seemed too hard. The goodies of the world seemed more attractive. You didn't completely forget God; maybe you even think warmly of the times you spent together. Or maybe you still spend some time together, but it just doesn't seem the same as when you first knew Him.

Those are all signs you're feeling thirsty. Life without God is dry, empty, and sometimes seems so worthless. By giving you a desire to taste of His spring, your Father's reminding you just how wonderful your fellowship was; no earthly rewards can take its place.

As the thirsty ones come to drink, they not only receive water. The gift of God's mercy provides them with extravagant blessings, symbolized by wine and milk. You can't pay for such blessings—God doesn't need your money. But He does want your love; that's why He went seeking about you.

If you're feeling thirsty, come to the water and drink deeply. Your Father holds the cup in His hand.

Pamela McQuade
Daily Wisdom for the Workplace

The Blessings of Forgiveness

Get rid of all bitterness, rage and anger, brawling and slander, along with every form of malice. Be kind and compassionate to one another, forgiving each other, just as in Christ God forgave you.

EPHESIANS 4:31–32 NIV

We all say and do stupid things sometimes. Generalizing the human condition like that helps me not to take things so personally. Everyone has an off day at times. I value friends who will remember that about me, and I afford them the same consideration.

But what about those times when someone does attack us personally? How do you just let it go? This happened to me one evening in the form of an e-mail. I was enraged and felt falsely accused. To burn off some bad energy, I headed outside for a walk. As I stomped down the road, I saw something lying in the gravel. It was the bottom half of a dirty plastic miniature, Barbie-like doll. The thought immediately came to me, "Don't lose your head!" I picked her up and took her home with me and set her on my desk as a reminder to not let myself get so upset that I end up broken and useless.

Forgiveness is a gift to us. It doesn't mean that what the offender did was okay. It doesn't mean we are weak. In fact, sometimes it takes a lot of strength to forgive someone who has wronged you. What it does mean is that we can go on with our lives without hanging on to bitterness, rage, and anger.

Julie Hufstetler
Singer, Songwriter

Rest

*"The Israelites are to observe the Sabbath. . . . It will
be a sign between me and the Israelites forever. . . ."
When the LORD finished speaking to Moses on
Mount Sinai, he gave him the two tablets of the
Testimony, the tablets of stone inscribed by the
finger of God.*

EXODUS 31:16–18 NIV

Wow, the Sabbath was serious business! This
passage makes it clear that it wasn't just tradition
or ceremony that caused the Israelites to rest on
the seventh day—these rules were written with
"the finger of God." Can you imagine what it
would be like if we still observed Old Testament
law in modern evangelical society? Most of us
would be six feet under!

I'm so thankful Jesus redeemed us from the

Law and we don't have to fear being zapped for mowing the lawn on Sunday. However, I also think we've thrown the baby out with the bathwater by ignoring the reason God stipulated a rest day in the first place. And we've paid the price in peace.

God's Word reveals that He rested, commanded His children to rest, declared that the land needed rest, made provisions for unwitting criminals to rest, and even planned a yearlong party to celebrate rest.

Rest wasn't negotiable for the Israelites, nor should it be for Christians. It's as clear a command from God as the Big Ten. The Sabbath isn't some punitive decree from a megalomaniac trying to take all the fun out of gardening on Sunday; it's God's merciful allowance for our protection.

Lisa Harper
Holding Out for a Hero

Blessed Assistance

All will go well for you, and your burden will be lifted.

ISAIAH 10:27 CEV

How tender our God is. How understanding, how patient, how caring.

The apostle Peter encourages us to "cast all your anxiety on him because he cares for you" (1 Peter 5:7 NIV). Jesus Himself invites all who are carrying heavy burdens to come to Him, and He promises to give them rest (see Matthew 11:28).

There is no mention of the size or shape of the burden. No problem is too small or insignificant and no burden too big or load too heavy. He knows us and how much weight we can carry. He is the Master Builder.

The scriptures tell us that He knows us by name (see Exodus 33:12), that the very hairs of our head are numbered (see Matthew 10:30), and that He not only sees our tears, but He cares so much that He gathers them and puts them in a bottle (see Psalm 56:8 KJV).

That is the God who walks with us and helps us carry our heavy loads. He knows our frames, our makeup, and our limitations. He remembers that we are frail, and He has promised not to give us more than we can take. This is the quiet knowing that we have as we carry our individual burdens through life.

Gigi Graham Tchividjian
A Quiet Knowing

The Gentleness of Christ

Thy gentleness hath made me great.

PSALM 18:35 KJV

The Gospels are full of Christ's tenderness. There is not room here even for the bare mention of the instances of it.

Let us glance at the volume of our own experience. Who that has had any dealings with Christ at all, but must bear witness that He has indeed dealt gently with us. What if He had ever "dealt with us after our sins"! But He never did, and never will. He hath dealt gently, and will deal gently with us, for His own sake, and according to His own heart, from the first drawings of His loving-kindness, on throughout the measureless developments of His everlasting love. Not till we are in heaven shall we know the full meaning of

"Thy gentleness hath made me great."

May we not recognize a command in this, as well as a responsibility to follow the example of the "gentleness of Christ"? Perhaps next time we are tempted to be a little harsh or hasty with an erring or offending one, the whisper will come, "Deal gently, for My sake!"

Frances Ridley Havergal
Daily Thoughts for the King's Children

Blessed Compassion

"I feel sorry for these people. They have been here with me for three days, and they have nothing left to eat."

MARK 8:2 NLT

It's easy to grow so self-centered that we don't look past our own problems or pain. Do we respond like Jesus did when faced with people in obvious distress and confusion? Jesus had been teaching and healing in the towns and villages of Galilee. At this time, a huge crowd had been with Jesus for three days, and they ran out of food. "I feel sorry for these people," the Lord said. "They have been here with me for three days, and they have nothing left to eat."

Jesus felt sorry—He felt what we would call "pity" or "compassion." Jesus had a shepherd's heart that was moved as He observed the crowds of people around Him who needed a "shepherd" to lead and guide them. Someone has defined compassion as "your hurt in my heart." Jesus definitely took the hurt of people into His heart.

Perhaps you object to His challenge to care compassionately for others. Maybe you think you have too many hurts of your own. Yet the Lord heals our own hurts as we reach out to attend to the hurts of others.

Jesus feels people's hurt in His heart, and He is in my heart—so guess what happens: Their hurt is in my heart! Once we feel great compassion for others, we will discover a great motivating force that will move us to compassionate action.

Jill Briscoe
The One Year Book of Devotions for Women

True Love

Love is patient, love is kind. It does not envy, it does not boast, it is not proud. It is not rude, it is not self-seeking, it is not easily angered, it keeps no record of wrongs. Love does not delight in evil but rejoices with the truth. It always protects, always trusts, always hopes, always perseveres.

1 Corinthians 13:4–7 niv

*L*ove interprets things in favor of the one loved. I had a long way to go to learn that, but the principle is clear enough in Paul's description: "Love is patient. . .never selfish, not quick to take offence. Love keeps no score of wrongs. . . . There is nothing love cannot face; there is no limit to its faith, its hope, and its endurance."

The trouble, of course, is that we must learn to love people. People are sinners. Love must be patient when it is tempted (by the delays of other people) to be impatient. Love must not be selfish, if other people are. Love does not take offence, though people are offensive sometimes. There are wrongs, but love won't keep score. There are things to be faced—but nothing love can't face—things to try love's faith, discourage its hope, and call for its endurance; but it keeps right on trusting, hoping, and enduring. Love never ends.

Elisabeth Elliot
Passion and Purity

The Gate to God

*"Enter through the narrow gate. For wide is the gate
and broad is the road that leads to destruction,
and many enter through it. But small is the gate and
narrow the road that leads to life, and only a few find it."*

MATTHEW 7:13–14 NIV

This tells me that what appears right, popular,
and sanctioned by man, may not be approved by
God. The gate may be open, the traffic may be
heavy, the people may be convincing, but they are
entering the wrong gate.

It isn't that God has posted a PRIVATE
ROAD—NO ACCESS sign. It's that few are willing
to enter through the gate of Christ. The cost of
relinquishment and obedience is too pricey for
them.

Our community recently conducted a tour of
exceptional homes. Many who wanted to see the

homes didn't because they were unwilling to pay the entrance fee. They were interested but not enough to relinquish their fifteen dollars at the gate. What a shame—there is nothing like entering in.

Jesus is our gate, for he gives us entrance to the Father. The Holy Spirit then begins to post road signs (via scripture, witnesses, promptings, etc.) to give us the guidance we need to stay on the road of righteousness. Now we have reason to celebrate, for no matter how unpopular our road, no matter how treacherous it becomes, we know we are not alone, and we have entered at the right (narrow) gate.

Patsy Clairmont
The Joyful Journey

No Surprises

*God can do anything, you know—far more than
you could ever imagine or guess or request in your
wildest dreams! He does it not by pushing us around
but by working within us, his Spirit deeply and
gently within us.*

EPHESIANS 3:20–21 MSG

As a child growing up in the late 1960s, the
classic television sitcoms are embedded in my
memory. There was innocence about them and
the guarantee that everything would turn out
okay by the end of the episode.

One such character that seemed to always
land on his feet was Gomer Pyle. The lovable,
gullible man-child from Mayberry that made his
way into the United States Marine Corps. His
optimism was infectious and his "luck" always

seemed to pay off in the end.

As I have faced challenges great and small, I am so often amazed by how God takes care of every detail. Even those I'm not aware of at the time. Whereas Gomer would state his famous, "Surprise, surprise, surprise," as a blessing would flow his way, when God reveals a solution I find myself saying, "Why am I surprised? My Father is faithful to His promises."

I believe that we are not to be surprised by the fact that God does amazing things. His resources and unconditional love are without limit. He simply asks us to embrace by faith the truth that He wants to meet our needs and He has some incredibly creative ways to accomplish His purposes through our lives.

Lisa Troyer
Circle of Friends

Blessed Harmony

*Therefore, my beloved brethren whom I long to see,
my joy and crown, in this way stand firm in the
Lord, my beloved. I urge Euodia and I urge
Syntyche to live in harmony in the Lord.*

PHILIPPIANS 4:1–2 NASB

Church committee meetings can either be a
blessing or a bear, depending, of course, upon
whether the members are working together for a
common goal. Evidently, two of the church women
at Philippi, Euodia and Syntyche, were less than
harmonious. Therefore, Paul admonished them.

It is significant that Paul took the time to
address this issue. Left unchecked, such arguing
would wreak havoc in the church. Perhaps you
have encountered someone who, although
she professes belief in Christ, has

treated you without charity or love. Fast, pray for guidance, and then go to her and pray again. Failure to do so gives Satan an opportunity to get a foothold within the church, as the argument escalates and people choose sides.

Speaking like a proud father, Paul refers to these believers at Philippi as his "joy and crown." He brought the gospel message to them. And then he stood back to watch them grow in their faith. He doesn't want it all to turn to ashes.

Carol L. Fitzpatrick
Daily Wisdom for Women

Blessed at Work

Commit your work to the Lord,
and your plans will be established.

PROVERBS 16:3 NRSV

For what has God fashioned you? If you're not sure, pray for guidance, with a mind open to accept whatever the Lord tells you. God's direction must persistently be petitioned since today's work may merely be the training ground for the job we have yet to discover.

Once you have prayed and heard God's direction, have the courage to walk where He leads. Tap into the power of commitment, keeping your course steady so that you will be amply rewarded, now and at the end of your journey.

To help you interact with coworkers in a Christlike way, pray for the power to live by God's Word. This will enable you to avoid four worldly traps, the first being the tendency to compare your job with those of others.

Second, don't let the daily grind of routine crush your spirit. Don't let the monotony of life get you down, but keep God first in your life.

Third, don't become so immersed in your present job that you miss the opportunities God puts in your path. If you're too involved in your current job, you may miss His promptings.

Finally, don't work just for the money. We must beware of having our eyes on the wrong treasure. Put your heart and soul into whatever you set your hand to, doing it to serve others and God.

Daily commit your work to God and consistently seek His direction. Remember that He opens doors for His children—but keep your eyes open to opportunity.

Donna K. Maltese
Power Prayers to Start Your Day

He Knows My Name

Fear not, for I have redeemed you; I have summoned you by name; you are mine.

ISAIAH 43:1 NIV

My mother was little more than a child herself when, at age seventeen, she gave birth to me. Not only was she young, she was crippled and unmarried. In scribbled handwriting, from the back room of my grandparents' home in Dallas, Texas, she wrote "Baby Girl Morris" on my birth certificate. However, she called me "Thelma" after the midwife who helped deliver me. Later I assumed the distinctive last name of "Smith."

Not many women can say, "I was a girl without a name," but I meet ladies every day who have no idea who they really are. It is one of the greatest privileges of my life to be able to say. . .Girl, have I

got good news for you!

One aspect of sharing God's love with women that I most enjoy is helping them regain their self-esteem. I get so excited as I am able to "midwife" them into an understanding of God's role in erasing the baggage of shame and guilt they may be dragging around. I tell them, "You don't have to live with silent, private guilt all of your life. What may have happened in your past is over and should be done with. It's history. You can pack your guilt and shame away in a box, use duct tape around the edges to seal it tightly, and put it in the trash where it belongs, because Jesus wants you to bring it to Him."

Thelma Wells
Kisses of Sunshine for Women

Known Facts

*All Scripture is inspired by God and profitable for
teaching, for reproof, for correction, for training
in righteousness; so that the man of God may be
adequate, equipped for every good work.*

2 Timothy 3:16–17 nasb

It is of vital importance for us to understand
that the Bible is a statement, not of theories, but
of actual facts; and that things are not true because they are in the Bible, but they are only in the
Bible because they are true.

A little boy, who had been studying at school
about the discovery of America, said to his father
one day, "Father, if I had been Columbus I would
not have taken all that trouble to discover
America."

"Why, what would you have

done?" asked the father.

"Oh," replied the little boy, "I would have just gone to the map and found it." This little boy did not understand that maps are only pictures of already known places, and that America did not exist because it was on the map, but it could not be on the map until it was already known to exist.

And similarly with the Bible. It is, like the map, a simple statement of facts; so that when it tells us that God loves us, it is only telling us something that is a fact, and that would not be in the Bible if it had not been already known to be a fact.

Hannah Whitall Smith
The God of All Comfort

The Blessings of Aging

"I kept thinking, 'Experience will tell.
The longer you live, the wiser you become.'"

JOB 32:7 MSG

Bible teacher Darlene Bishop once said, "God called me to teach the Word when I was only fourteen years old. I knew it. I heard that still small voice. But I didn't preach my first sermon until I was thirty-eight years old." She went on to say that she's now in her early sixties, and she's more effective for God than she's ever been before.

Today's society would have you believe that women past thirty should be put out to pasture. But that's simply not the case. God isn't concerned about our age, our wrinkles, or any gray hairs that might be sprouting. He just needs a willing vessel with a faithful heart.

Take Sarah in the Bible, for example. Abraham's wife thought she was too old to bear Abraham an heir. By the world's standards, she was well past childbearing years. Physically, it was impossible for her to conceive a child. But God had given her and Abraham a promise—that Abraham would be the father of many nations. God didn't need Sarah's youthful body to produce a child. God just needed her faith and her willingness to be used. Once those were in place, she birthed Isaac—the promised heir.

Maybe you look into the mirror and see a woman who is too old to do anything worthwhile. You are not too old to do what God has planned for you. Like Darlene, you may be entering into your greatest days.

Michelle Medlock Adams
Secrets of Beauty

Jesus' Prayers

Christ Jesus, who died—more than that,
who was raised to life—is at the right hand
of God and is also interceding for us.

ROMANS 8:34 NIV

Several years ago I visited with an older woman who I knew from childhood. She knew my family and the difficult dynamics, as well as my husband's family of origin. My husband had grandparents who prayed fervently for their children and grandchildren. As we talked together about my husband and I serving the Lord, she looked at me and asked, "Jocelyn, I know who was praying for Bruce. But who was praying for you?"

I left her house but her question remained in my mind. Several days later as I read Romans 8, the Lord answered our question. The words hit me like a ton of bricks: It was Jesus. All those years of aimless wandering, little sense of purpose and worth, dumb decisions and pain. He was the One praying for me the entire time. He was the One talking to the Father on my behalf reminding Him that the price of my sin had been paid. He was the One asking for mercy, grace, and protection as I stumbled in utter confusion. He was the One who saw and declared the future and hope that lay ahead.

Jesus is praying for us. Be encouraged no matter the circumstance. We have the greatest prayer partner we could ever want. Jesus Christ, King of kings and Lord of lords, is praying for you today.

Jocelyn Hamsher
Circle of Friends

Total Peace

You will keep in perfect peace all who trust in you.

ISAIAH 26:3 NLT

Many people see their emotional state with resignation: "This is just the way I am" or "I guess I'll have to live with it because this is as good as it gets." Others believe that while there may be a way to make essential changes, one has to be either very spiritual or wealthy enough to afford the best professional help. "Emotional health," one girl told me, "is a remote ideal that many people want but very few people achieve."

My definition of emotional health is having total peace about who you are, what you're doing, and where you're going, both individually and in relationship to those around you. In other words, it's feeling totally at peace about the past, present, and future of your life. It's knowing you're in line with God's ultimate purpose for you and being fulfilled in that. When you have that kind of peace and you no longer live in emotional agony, you are a success.

Stormie Omartian
Finding Peace for Your Heart

Used by God

"But the Holy Spirit will come upon you and give you power. Then you will tell everyone about me in Jerusalem, in all Judea, in Samaria, and everywhere in the world."

ACTS 1:8 CEV

We are not all called to be the King's ambassadors, but all who have heard the messages of salvation for themselves are called to be "the Lord's messengers," and day by day, as He gives us opportunity, we are to deliver "the Lord's message" unto the people.

He who made every power can use every power—memory, judgment, imagination, quickness of apprehension or insight; specialties of musical, poetical, oratorical, or artistic faculty; special tastes for reasoning, philosophy, history, natural science, or natural history—all these may be dedicated to Him, sanctified by Him, and used by Him. Whatever He has given, He will use, if we will let Him. Often, in the most unexpected ways, and at the most unexpected turns, something read or acquired long ago suddenly comes into use.

We cannot foresee what will thus "come in useful"; but He knew, when He guided us to learn it, what would be wanted for in His service. So may we not ask Him to bring His perfect foreknowledge to bear on all our mental training and storing? To guide us to read or study exactly what He knows there will be use for in the work to which He has called or will call us?

Frances Ridley Havergal
Kept for the Master's Use

Courage

Be strong and let your heart take courage,
all you who hope in the LORD.

PSALM 31:24 NASB

There are many places, my child, where only sheer courage will see you through. Prayer is the breath of the soul. Faith is paramount. Love is the essence of pure being. But none of these will suffice in the hour of stress if you have not courage.

Courage is that inner fortification of the disposition that is undaunted by the impossible, unthwarted by the improbable, and undismayed by the unthinkable. Courage makes perseverance attainable when encouragement is nowhere to be found. Courage is a stream of cool water to the soul when life is dry and parched. Courage gives stamina when love is gone, faith is wavering, and prayer is difficult.

Courage rises like the delivering angel out of the deep unshaken assurance of the immutability of the character and faithfulness of God. Courage knows that for the child of God there is no such thing as disaster. Courage keeps the destination in view and heeds not the intervening obstacles. Courage does not count the cost neither laments losses, because it reckons on unfailing supply and is content in knowing that one man's loss is another man's gain and rejoices as much in one as in the other.

Courage is self-denying, self-effacing, self-repudiating, self-sacrificing. Courage is the simplicity of knowing: God is working out His purposes through every circumstance of my life. His plan is good, and how He chooses to act is none of my business, and whom He uses to bring it about is not my concern.

Frances J. Roberts
Make Haste My Beloved

A Blessed Attitude

*And whatever you do, whether in word or deed,
do it all in the name of the Lord Jesus, giving thanks
to God the Father through him.*

I am not an early riser. No matter how much sleep I seem to get, getting out of my nice soft bed is always a chore. I have to force myself to put my feet on the floor. Except on the days when I can sleep in. Then I wake early and cannot go back to sleep!

Attitude is everything. Every day we face all sorts of mundane, reoccurring tasks that can become little irritants in our life, if we let them. Dishes, scrubbing the bathroom, driving in traffic, getting groceries, picking up things around the house, going to work, dealing with coworkers—we go about our daily living and usually we just do it without too much thought. If you're like me, sometimes we do it with an attitude—the wrong attitude.

We complain, we're grouchy with our families, irritated with our coworkers; we think, if not say aloud, "It's not fair."

God's Word tells us to do, whatever we do, for Him and His glory (1 Corinthians 10:31). Philippians 4:13 tells us we can do anything through Christ and by His strength. And Colossians 3:23 (NKJV) says, "Whatever you do, do it heartily, as to the Lord and not to men."

It seems pretty simple then: Our strength to do anything comes from Him, and whatever we do is for Him and to make His glory known. Even in the little things.

Missy Horsfall
Circle of Friends

The Blessings of Remembering

Then they believed His words; they sang His praise.
They soon forgot His works.

*H*ave you ever known a weakening in the inward places of your soul because you had let slip the memory of what your God did in the past? You had believed His words, you had sung His praises, for in very truth you had seen His words fulfilled. And then, somehow, the memory faded, blotted out by a disappointment perhaps, and you "forgot His works."

I have known this to happen, and I have proved that after such forgetfulness prayer becomes less adventurous, less brave in faith and expectation. We ask for the smaller rather than the greater things, and then (as in the story from which I am quoting) "leanness" enters into the soul.

May the Lord, by His Spirit, quicken our memories, and help us to do our part by gathering up the forces of memory. It is worthwhile to do anything that will help us do this. "We will remember Thy love" (Song of Solomon 1:4 KJV) and all the ways the Lord our God has led us.

Amy Carmichael
Edges of His Ways

No Need to Worry

"Therefore do not worry about tomorrow, for tomorrow will worry about its own things. Sufficient for the day is its own trouble."

MATTHEW 6:34 NKJV

It is when we find ourselves in these hard places that we make the choice to worry or worship. When we worry, we feel we have to come up with justifications and careful explanations for the naysayers. When we worry, we listen to the voices of Acceptance and Rejection. When we worry, we lie awake at night and ponder Satan's lies. When we worry, we have pity parties where the guests of honor are Negative Thinking, Doubt, and Resignation.

But we can make the choice to worship. When we worship in these hard places, we are reminded that none of this is about us—it is all about God. We turn our focus off ourselves and back onto God Almighty. God can use empty places in your life to draw your heart to Him. He is the great love of your life who will never disappoint. He is building your eternal home that will never get broken, dirty, or need redecorating. He is preparing a place of eternal perfect fellowship.

We all worship something. We must choose whom—or what—we will worship. Will it be the opinions of others, our fears, or even our own comfort? Or will it be the One who created our souls to worship? Whatever we worship, we will obey. As we choose to be radically obedient to the Lord, we must be radical about choosing to worship Him and Him alone.

Lysa TerKeurst
Radically Obedient, Radically Blessed

He Is

*And without faith it is impossible to please Him,
for he who comes to God must believe that He is and
that He is a rewarder of those who seek Him.*

HEBREWS 11:6 NASB

*B*elieve that He is. This is the challenge that
God lays out for us in this particular portion of
scripture. As believers in Christ, we must learn
to walk in this profound truth on a moment-by-
moment basis, every day. As a woman of God,
appointed to various assignments in this season
of life, it is my desire that I might fully grasp the
truth that He is.

When life feels overwhelming. When my
calendar is full. When the circumstances of
life serve us heartache and profound grief.
When we find ourselves bound in a

tangle of sin and consequences. He is. In that moment of choice, will we choose to have faith and believe that God will be all that we need?

He is enough. He is the all-sufficient One. He is my Rock. He is my Redeemer. He is Truth. He is the One who lifts my head. This is who God is, in every circumstance, every day. He is.

How am I to respond to who He is? I am to exercise faith and simply come. I am to believe Him and seek Him. God does His part by doing and being everything He has ever promised. We do our part by choosing faith and diligently seeking. And what is the result? The *is* of God becomes increasingly alive in us, and there is great reward.

Elizabeth Ward
Circle of Friends

Trust

And Mary said, Yes, I see it all now: I'm the Lord's
maid, ready to serve. Let it be with me
just as you say. Then the angel left her.

LUKE 1:38 MSG

I wish I could be more like Mary every day. My
heart longs to trust God the way she did—ready
to serve, no matter what the gossip, the criticism,
and the misunderstanding from others, in spite of
the ache in my soul every time I think of my son. I
long to pray with an honest heart, "Be it unto me
according to thy word" (Luke 1:38 KJV).

I read her poignant words and think, Wow.
How could she do it? How could she be so wise?
So trusting? So surrendered? Was it by her youth?
Her shock? The result of a lifelong, intimate
dependence on God? It's almost too much to

comprehend. I find myself with questions—big questions. Do I even want to say that to God when the consequences could be so painful? Do I want to get to a place when I give Him that much power? Do I really understand that He already has that power and that my resistance only hurts myself?

Perhaps one day I will learn to trust Him as completely as Mary did.

Carol Kent
A New Kind of Normal

Abiding in His Love

"As the Father has loved me, so have I loved you."

JOHN 15:9 NIV

When will we get through our heads how loved we are? Try to grasp this truth as tightly as you can: Christ Jesus loves you like the Father loves Him. He loves you like His only begotten— as if you were the only one!

Christ follows His statement with a command in the same verse: "Now remain in my love." I love the New King James word for "remain"—*abide*. The term means exactly what it implies: dwell in His love, remain in it, tarry in it, soak in it. For heaven's sake, live in it! How do we do such a thing?

Let me paraphrase what I think Christ is saying in this passage. Please put your name in the blanks:

My love for you, _____, is perfect, divine, and lavish beyond your imagination and far beyond your soul's cavernous needs. In fact, I love you like My Father loves Me, and I am the only begotten Son and the uncontested apple of His eye. _____, My love for you is as constant as an ever-surging fountain, but you don't always sense it because you move in and out of the awareness of My presence. My desire is for you to pitch your mobile home so intimately close to Me that you are never outside the keen awareness of My extravagant love.

Beth Moore
The Beloved Disciple

The Promiser

God is not a man, so he does not lie. He is not human, so he does not change his mind. Has he ever spoken and failed to act? Has he ever promised and not carried it through?

NUMBERS 23:19 NLT

It is grand to trust in the promises, but it is grander still to trust in the Promiser. The promises may be misunderstood or misapplied, and at the moment when we are leaning all our weight upon them, they may seem utterly to fail us. But no one ever trusted in the Promiser and was confounded.

The God who is behind His promises and is infinitely greater than His promises can never fail us in any emergency, and the soul that is stayed on Him cannot know anything but perfect peace.

The little child does not always understand its mother's promises, but it knows its mother, and its childlike trust is founded not on her word, but upon herself. And just so it is with those of us who have learned the lesson of this "Although" and "Yet."

There may not be a prayer answered or a promise fulfilled to our own consciousness, but what of that? Behind the prayers and behind the promises, there is God, and He is enough. And to such a soul the simple words, GOD IS, answer every question and solve every doubt.

Hannah Whitall Smith
The Christian's Secret of a Happy Life

Known and Loved

"And even the very hairs of your head are all numbered."

MATTHEW 10:30 NIV

God knows how many hairs are on my head, and He knows everything about every single hair on my head. He knows which ones will turn gray and when, which ones have split ends, which ones will come out in the shower tomorrow. Not just because He is God and He knows everything, but because He knows me.

When I think about moments I have felt so overwhelmingly loved, they're moments where I've felt known. Like when I was a kid and my dad bought just the right brand of cheese puffs because he knew the ones I didn't like. Or when my mom tells me she's praying for me to have patience with others because she knows how black and white I see things. Or when my husband automatically grabs my hand without me asking on icy parking lots or skinny stairwells because he knows how klutzy I am and how easily I fall. These are moments where I know I'm loved because of how well others know me.

God knows more about me than anyone ever could, because He made every part of me. It's not just the number of hairs on my head or the number of cells in my body. It's my hurts, my hopes, my failures, my triumphs, my strengths, and my weaknesses. And being that known means that He loves me like nothing else I'll ever experience.

Emily Smith
Circle of Friends

The Blessing of Availability

There are different kinds of gifts, but the same Spirit. There are different kinds of service, but the same Lord. There are different kinds of working, but the same God works all of them in all men.

1 CORINTHIANS 12:4–6 NIV

It's painfully easy to spot a woman who lacks a sense of mission. She's running as fast as she can, but it's never fast enough. She allows everyone else to set her priorities. Her husband wants her to take up bowling. Her children want her to chauffeur them from cheerleading, to gymnastics, to the mall, to Susie's house. (And that's just Monday.) The missions committee wants her to plan the fall conference. A friend wants her to join aerobics. Another friend recruited her for the choir. And on and on and on.

These activities are all wonderful, provided you do them in response to God's calling upon your life. However, if your primary motivation is winning the approval of others, trouble waits ahead. If you hunger for man's approval, you'll find it almost impossible to say no to any request for your time. Unfortunately, very often when you're saying yes to people, you're saying no to God.

We've said it before, but we can't emphasize it enough. God doesn't want us to do anything for Him. He doesn't need our help or suggestions. He wants us to be available so He can do His work through us.

Donna Partow
Becoming a Vessel God Can Use

The Gift of Rest

*"Come to me, all you who are weary and burdened,
and I will give you rest. Take my yoke upon you and
learn from me, for I am gentle and humble in heart,
and you will find rest for your souls."*

MATTHEW 11:28–29 NIV

For years, I found little time to rest. As a
full-time caregiver with an active outside ministry, my time and energy were spread dangerously
thin. Rest was a luxury I hoped for one day. Big
mistake, I learned when my physical, emotional,
and even spiritual health dried right up.

Regular rest mattered a lot to Jesus. No one
has ever been busier, had a greater task to do in a
short amount of time, or been more important,
including any sitting president or pope.
And yet, Jesus took time to rest and

to commune with His heavenly Father and His friends. But He practiced a different kind of rest, something so obvious I had missed it.

Jesus found rest in an inner posture of submission, a poised oneness in body, mind, and soul with His Father's will. That can't happen reading a devotional for five or ten minutes a day, but in regularly withdrawing to be alone with God.

Could I do that? Can you? Trust me, the alternative isn't good.

What matters more than being fresh for God's will today, being all His, saturated with His holy Presence? He knows we need rest and renewal right down to our toes. When I forget, His love stops me and carries me to a quiet place to drink deeply and remember again.

Virelle Kidder
Meet Me at the Well

Staying Connected

I am the vine, ye are the branches: He that abideth in me, and I in him, the same bringeth forth much fruit: for without me ye can do nothing.

JOHN 15:5 KJV

Are you "connected"? You may have a cell phone, beeper, computer, and a thousand other gadgets, but that doesn't mean you have the right connection.

Jesus talked about having the one everyone needs: a connection with God. When we're tapped into God the way a branch taps into a vine, we've got an attachment that does more for us than any phone, beeper, or computer.

Can you use your cell phone from anywhere in the world? Probably not. Some places it just can't receive transmissions. But you can always reach

God in prayer—more than that, you'll get an answer, not an answering machine. You don't have to wait for a call back, either. And unlike a beeper user, God won't forget to pick up the message.

Computers are wonderful machines, but not as wonderful as God. From them you can get a lot of information, and with them you can bring forth a lot of work, but they will not give you all truth. They can help you do a lot, but you'd never say you can do nothing without them.

Connect with Jesus today, and you'll surpass all technology has to offer.

Pamela McQuade
Daily Wisdom for the Workplace

The Blessing of Broken Dreams

"No eye has seen, no ear has heard, no mind has conceived what God has prepared for those who love him."

1 CORINTHIANS 2:9 NIV

My Bible lay open to the Song of Songs, a book that some say can be seen as Jesus pursuing His bride, the church. On this day I chose to read it as if I were reading a love story of Jesus pursuing me as His bride. This became even more real to me as I read the words in chapter 2, verse 1.

"I am a rose of Sharon," the woman said to her beloved.

"What is your name?" God seemed to ask.

"Lord, my name is Sharon," I whispered aloud.

"Look it up," He prompted my heart.

I went to my Bible dictionary and I looked up *Sharon*. Tears filled my eyes as I discovered that Sharon was a fertile valley near Mount Carmel. You see, in my medical chart, somewhere among the diagnosis and prognosis of years of testing, is written the word *infertile*. And yet God made sure that my name meant "fertile" before I was even born.

No, I don't have a house full of children with my blood coursing through their veins, but God did make my dreams come true. Through the ministry of writing and speaking, I have spiritual children all around the world! When we give our broken dreams to God, He fashions them into a beautiful mosaic that is lovelier than anything we could have ever imagined.

Sharon Jaynes
Extraordinary Moments with God

Blessed Grace

"You intended to harm me, but God intended it for good to accomplish what is now being done, the saving of many lives."

GENESIS 50:20 NIV

One day recently something lit a fuse of anger in someone who then burned me with hot words. I felt sure I didn't deserve this response, but when I ran to God about it, He reminded me of part of a prayer I'd been using lately: "Teach me to treat all that comes to me with peace of soul and with firm conviction that Your will governs all."

Where could that kind of peace come from? Only from God, who gives "not as the world gives."

His will that I should be burned?

Here we must tread softly. His will

governs all. In a wrong-filled world we suffer (and cause) many a wrong. God is here to heal and comfort and forgive. He who brought blessing to many out of the sin of the jealous brothers against Joseph means this hurt for my ultimate blessing and, I think, for an increase of love between me and the one who hurt me. Love is very patient, very kind. Love never seeks its own. Love looks to God for His grace to help.

Elisabeth Elliot
Keep a Quiet Heart

Pardon Me, But Your Imperfection Is Showing

*But God chose the foolish things of the world
to shame the wise; God chose the weak things of the
world to shame the strong.*

1 CORINTHIANS 1:27 NIV

If I had a theme verse, I'd probably choose the part of Paul's letter to the church at Corinth in which he says that God deliberately chooses things the world considers foolish and weak in order to shame those who think they're really something. The bottom line (no pun intended) is that I'm the poster child for imperfection—every time I turn around, my flaws are revealed with a flourish!

One afternoon, when I was walking back toward my office from the restroom, I ran into a gentleman who worked in the department across from mine. We stood in there in the hallway for a while—talking about God's sovereignty and how He orders our steps.

It was a wonderful conversation, except for one little detail: The whole time we were talking this guy wouldn't look directly at me.

When we finished our conversation a few minutes later, I felt a little draft, glanced down, and was horrified to see that I'd accidentally tucked my skirt into my underwear when I was in the restroom!

I'm sure you have a few of your own embarrassing stories, moments when your weakness was more apparent than your winsomeness. The good news of the gospel that Paul reiterates in this book is that God is well aware of our blemishes. He's not surprised by our shortcomings. Miraculously, He cherishes us anyway.

Lisa Harper
What the Bible Is All About for Women

Beauty

*And God saw every thing that he had made,
and, behold, it was very good.*

GENESIS 1:31 KJV

A thing of beauty is a rose in full bloom. What
a pleasure to hold in the hand a perfect rose and
admire its soft, velvety petals, to smell of its rich
fragrance, and to feast upon its beauty of color-
ing! One would be tempted to say, "In this nature
has done her best." But nature, and the God of nature, gave us many beautiful and glorious things.

The grown woman who stands just at the door
of life's responsibilities, ready to enter in upon
her life work, represents powers and possibilities
unbounded. Her influence in the world is sure to
go on down to the end of time. It is impossible that
she should live entirely for and to herself.

First is her influence upon womankind. There are none of us so weak and insignificant but that someone will pattern after us, or draw courage from us. By our trueness to principle, our loyalty to right and truth, we can each be a stay and fortress to the weaker sisters about us. In the home, in the neighborhood, in the congregation, everywhere, a good woman is a mighty force among women.

Mabel Hale
Beautiful Girlhood

The Cardinal Reminder

Is there any place I can go to. . .be out of your sight? If I climb to the sky, you're there! If I go underground, you're there! If I flew on morning's wings to the far western horizon, You'd find me in a minute—you're already there waiting!

PSALM 139:7–10 MSG

I sat in my living room chair gazing out the window. I lamented to the Lord, asking Him where He was in that particular season of life. I felt as though my prayers bounced off the ceiling and that I was totally alone.

As I sat there, the most beautiful cardinal came and sat on the railing right outside my window. The moment it perched, I was reminded that God had been beside me the entire time. One of the ways our Father reveals Himself is through the beauty of His creation—it speaks of His glory and His Presence. That morning, God spoke through a beautiful red bird simply to say, "I am here."

Over the next while, I spotted cardinals everywhere, while driving and out on walks. Every time, I was reminded of His love and comforted knowing He was with me—that the Earth was filled with Him. There is nowhere that I can go that He is not present.

The "cardinal reminder" is for all of us. We are not walking alone. We have been made a promise as God's daughters that He will never let us down. He will never walk off and leave us. No matter what seasons we walk through, He is there to hold our hand.

Jocelyn Hamsher
Circle of Friends

Honored by God

It came about in due time, after Hannah had conceived, that she gave birth to a son; and she named him Samuel, saying, "Because I have asked him of the Lord."

1 Samuel 1:20 nasb

Hannah, a woman of real faith, wanted to keep her promise to God. After Samuel was born and she had weaned him, she took him promptly to the temple. There she said to Eli, " 'Oh, my lord! As your soul lives, my lord, I am the woman who stood here beside you, praying to the Lord. For this boy I prayed, and the Lord has given me my petition which I asked of Him. So I have also dedicated him to the Lord; as long as he lives he is dedicated to the Lord' " (1 Samuel 1:26–28 nasb).

Every year Hannah and Elkanah returned

for their sacrifice at the temple, and every year Hannah brought Samuel a new robe to wear. For her faithfulness, God blessed Hannah with three more sons and two daughters (1 Samuel 2:21).

God was now training Samuel to take over as judge of Israel, as Eli's own sons had no regard for the Lord. As Samuel continued to grow "in favor. . . with the LORD" (1 Samuel 2:26 NASB), the Lord declared, "'Those who honor me I will honor, but those who despise me will be disdained'" (1 Samuel 2:30 NIV).

Carol L. Fitzpatrick
Daily Wisdom for Women

Christ's Jewels

They are as the stones of a crown, sparkling in His land.

ZECHARIAH 9:16 NASB

It is when we are broken inside ourselves—through our defects—that we can give back the lovely hues of His light to others. It is then that the lamp of the temple can burn brightly within us and not flicker or go out.

Still, there will be times when we lose the luster in our lives and it is vital to know how to restore it. When silver or brass becomes tarnished, we get out the tarnish remover and do some rubbing. What can we do when we need to bring back the shine in our own lives? We can pause early in the day to seek God's guidance. We can count our blessings and name them one by one.

An attitude of gratitude rids our lives of the

film of frustration, the rust of resentment, and the varnish of vanity—all destroyers of self-esteem. When we count our blessings, we multiply harmony and good feelings, and the lamp's flame burns higher once again.

Without God's touch in our lives—His work in us to will and to do His good pleasure—there is no sparkle or scant joy. But when we allow Him to work within us—when we feel His hand upon us—we are no longer hidden treasures; we become sparkling jewels that beautify His kingdom.

Barbara Johnson
The Best of Barbara Johnson

Blessed Confidence

And Mary said: "My soul glorifies the Lord and my spirit rejoices in God my Savior, for he has been mindful of the humble state of his servant. From now on all generations will call me blessed."

LUKE 1:46–48 NIV

What if Mary had said no?

She could have. God didn't make her accept His will for her life; He let her choose. As overwhelming as the appearance of an angel in her room must have been, Mary's choice should not have been an easy one. Her life was simple and stable: She was young, engaged to a good man, and ready to start her own home. Accepting God's will for her meant risking all of that and much more.

Mary's mind, however, was on the

Lord, not human society. She stood in awe of such an honor, and asked only how God planned to achieve this miracle. Her love of God and understanding of scriptures gave her complete confidence in her unhesitant, "Yes, Lord!"

Mary was indeed blessed, but being Jesus' mother came with tremendous anxiety and heartache. She saw the glory of His miracles but also felt the pain of His death.

Mary could have said no, the same as any of us who feel God's tug on our lives. As Mary discovered, following God can lead us down a path filled with pain as well as joy. Yet if we love Him and understand His love for us, then we will discover the confidence to say "yes!"

Ramona Richards
Secrets of Confidence

"Daughter, I Am Here"

Your people did not conquer the land with their swords; they did not win it by their own power; it was by your power and your strength, by the assurance of your presence, which showed that you loved them.

Psalm 44:3 gnt

I remember when I was a little girl and found myself in any trouble or perplexity, the coming in of my father or mother on the scene would always bring me immediate relief. The moment I heard the voice of one of them saying, "Daughter, I am here," that moment every burden dropped off and every anxiety was stilled.

It was their simple presence that did it. They did not need to promise to relieve me, they did not need to tell me their plans of relief; the simple fact of their presence was all the assurance I required that everything now would be set straight and all would go well for me, and my only interest after their arrival was simply to see how they would do it all.

How often in the Bible He has stilled all questions and all fears by the simple announcement, "I will be with thee"; and who can doubt that in these words He meant to assure us that all His wisdom, and love, and omnipotent power would therefore, of course, be engaged on our side? I remember to this day the inspiring sense of utter security that used to come to me with my earthly father's presence. I never feared anything when he was by.

And surely with my heavenly Father by, there can be no possible room for fear.

Hannah Whitall Smith
The Christian's Secret of a Happy Life

Our Place Is in Christ

For you are my hiding place;
you protect me from trouble.

PSALM 32:7 NLT

Are you sure that you are in the place where you are called? In the office, at the engine, at the side of your husband? Jesus gives you your place. "Abide in me," He says, "and I in you. As the branch cannot bear fruit of itself, except it abide in the vine; no more can ye, except ye abide in me" (John 15:4 KJV). Your place is in Him.

There is no room and no time for our own plans to do private battle with the evil one, for a game with the chained-up lion, for coquetting with great or small sins of everyday life. With Jesus hid in God! Can we find a safer hiding place? The devil will have to go first through God and

Jesus before he reaches us!

When soldiers are trained, they receive their training in barracks together with others. The training in the victorious army of God for the last great battle does not take place under unusual circumstances, but in the midst of the common daily life. Here is the place of training—and everything we experience belongs to that training.

Corrie ten Boom
The End Battle

God's Word

But if I say, "I will not mention him or speak any more in his name," his word is in my heart like a fire, a fire shut up in my bones. I am weary of holding it in; indeed, I cannot.

JEREMIAH 20:9 NIV

As a child of God, it has been my prayer for many years that the Lord would give me an insatiable appetite for His Word. There were many times in my Christian life when I struggled to understand God's Word or make it a priority to spend time in it each day. I came to a place in my Christian walk where I confessed these challenges to the Lord. Humbling myself before our merciful God, I began to ask Him for a supernatural desire for His living Word.

Like the persistent knocker found

in Luke 11:8, our desire to know, love, and understand the Word of God should cause us to shake the "halls of heaven" with our persistent prayers. Through the grace and power of God, this verse in Jeremiah can become the reality of our hearts. As children of God, we can ask Him for His life-giving Word to fill us to such an extent that it becomes like a fire in our bones. Like Jeremiah, God can grow us to a place where we become weary if we don't speak of it or mention His name. Our God's living Word begs to take hold of us, to be life to us, and indwell us to such a degree that we cannot hold it in.

Elizabeth Ward
Circle of Friends

Blessed Ministry

"Come, follow me," Jesus said,
"and I will make you fishers of men."

MATTHEW 4:19 NIV

Walking beside the glistening blue waters of the Sea of Galilee, Jesus saw two brothers casting their fishing nets. When He spoke the words recorded above, Peter and Andrew must have been intrigued. But Jesus didn't invent the phrase "fishers of men." Philosophers and teachers of that day used this term to describe those who captured men's minds.

The passage goes on to say that Peter and Andrew immediately left their nets and followed Jesus. But this wasn't their first invitation to follow Him. They had gone with Jesus to Capernaum and Galilee and later returned to their trade of fishing. However, this particular invitation was to full-time ministry, and they responded whole-heartedly.

But why did Christ want these fishermen? Peter and Andrew were men of action who knew how to get a job done without quitting or complaining. Their tenacity would be an asset to Christ's ministry of soul winning.

Jesus came not only to save but to teach men and women how to have true servants' hearts. And the substance of ministry is service.

Carol L. Fitzpatrick
Daily Wisdom for Women

The Unending Gift of Love

"What does the LORD your God require of you?
He requires only that you fear the LORD your God,
and live in a way that pleases him, and love him
and serve him with all your heart and soul."

DEUTERONOMY 10:12 NLT

*H*e has created us to love. We have a sealed treasure of love, which either remains sealed and then gradually dries up and wastes away, or is unsealed and poured out, and yet is the fuller and not the emptier for the outpouring.

The more love we give, the more we have to give. So far it is only natural. But when the Holy Spirit reveals the love of Christ and sheds abroad the love of God in our hearts, this natural love is penetrated with a new principle, as it discovers a new Object. Everything that it beholds in that

Object gives it new depth and new colors. As it sees the holiness, the beauty, and the glory, it takes the deep hues of conscious sinfulness, unworthiness, and nothingness. As it sees even a glimpse of the love that passeth knowledge, it takes the glow of wonder and gratitude. And when it sees that love drawing close to its deepest need with blood-purchased pardon, it is intensified and stirred, and there is no more time for weighing and measuring; we must pour it out, all there is of it, with our tears, at the feet that were pierced for love of us.

Frances Ridley Havergal
Kept for the Master's Use

Our Wonderful Counselor

For to us a child is born, to us a son is given, and the government will be on his shoulders. And he will be called Wonderful Counselor, Mighty God, Everlasting Father, Prince of Peace.

ISAIAH 9:6 NIV

We can always talk to God, remembering that God has called us into fellowship with Jesus Christ our Lord (1 Corinthians 1:9). Do we consciously arrange time to receive His fellowship? When was the last time we offered Him ours? It is a strong temptation to run to the phone when we need advice or help of any kind, forgetting to seek first the living Word of God, whose ear is always open to our cry. Try the simple reminder of 2 Peter 2:9 (NIV), "The Lord knows how to rescue godly men from trials," or Psalm 57:1 (NIV), "Have mercy on me, O

God, have mercy on me, for in you my soul takes refuge. I will take refuge in the shadow of your wings until the disaster has passed."

When Christian, in *Pilgrim's Progress*, reached the hill of Calvary, "his burden loosed from off his shoulders, and fell from off his back, and began to tumble; and so continued to do, till it came to the mouth of the Sepulchre, where it fell in." The Bible teaches us that here is a Wonderful Counselor.

Elisabeth Elliot
Secure in the Everlasting Arms

Called to Minister

Whatever you do, work at it with all your heart,
as working for the Lord, not for men.

COLOSSIANS 3:23 NIV

Ministry is for every woman. It's not just a "call-ing" for pastors, missionaries, and evangelists.

Many years ago, God chose a woman named Miriam to be a prophetess and worship leader, helping her brothers Moses and Aaron in bring-ing the people of Israel out of their slavery in Egypt. God miraculously allowed the people to walk through the Red Sea on dry ground—and then caused the waters to wash away the pursuing Egyptian army (Exodus 14–15). After the safe crossing, Miriam led worship, "and all the women followed her, with tambourines and dancing. Miriam sang to them: 'Sing to the LORD, for he is highly exalted. The horse and its rider he has hurled into the sea' " (Exodus 15:20–21 NIV).

Effective ministry is not based on our abilities. We don't make it happen ourselves—we partner with God through prayer, and He provides the power. One of the best ways we can minister to others is by praying for them. It's not always easy, but it's always worth it.

When we pray for our ministry, we can ask God to give us the willingness and compassion to serve others. If we are not sure where to spend our time, we can ask God to help us identify our spiritual gifts and to use them effectively.

Jackie M. Johnson
Power Prayers for Women

Blessed Communication

*My dear brothers and sisters: You must all be quick
to listen, slow to speak, and slow to get angry.*

JAMES 1:19 NLT

Listening works wonders! Loving silence has
no sound but tells the one sitting next to you that
you care. It can say to the hurting heart, "I want to
free you to think about yourself, your failures, and
your goals. Because I love you and am interested
in you I am willing to sit in silence with you."

Can you sit with a friend without talking? Can
you sit with your husband in silence? Or do you,
as I tend to, complete all his sentences for him? I
am learning to use a short reply, because it invites
more response! I have thanked God that He has
graced me with a companion, and I have reminded
myself that he is indeed a companion and not a

competitor in a word game!

I have learned to listen and discover with joy the unusual and unique facets of the one I love. I pray hard to fight down my impulsive, emotional response and let him talk.

For this I need to rely on Jesus. I have discovered that God is delighted to tame my tongue and tune my ear; and whenever He has been allowed to do so, He has filled my heart with the knowledge that listening with love brings love in return!

Jill Briscoe
The One Year Book of Devotions for Women

The Blessing of Old Friends

A good name is rather to be chosen than great riches,
and loving favour rather than silver and gold.

When plans were being made to celebrate my eighty-fifth birthday in March, 1905, Mr. Cleveland wrote another beautiful letter, the text of which follows:

My dear friend:
It is more than fifty years ago that our acquaintance and friendship began; and ever since that time I have watched your continuous and disinterested labor in uplifting humanity, and pointing out the way to an appreciation of God's goodness and mercy.

Though these labors have, I know, brought you abundant rewards in your consciousness of good accomplished, those who have known of your works and sympathized with your noble purposes owe it to themselves that you are apprised of their remembrance of these things. I am, therefore, exceedingly gratified to learn that your eighty-fifth birthday is to be celebrated with a demonstration of this remembrance. As one proud to call you an old friend, I desire to be early in congratulating you on your long life of usefulness, and wishing you in the years yet to be added to you, the peace and comfort born of the love of God.

Yours very sincerely,
Grover Cleveland

Fanny Crosby
Memories of Eighty Years

Perfectly Loved

To all perfection I see a limit;
but your commands are boundless.

PSALM 119:96 NIV

Do you know the problem with trying to be perfect? You always end up disappointed in yourself and others, because no matter how hard you try, you'll never be perfect.

That's not a negative confession, it's just reality—which is why being a perfectionist is so frustrating. Once you understand that perfection is only a goal—not a requirement—you will be a lot happier in all that you do.

Go ahead and shoot for perfection, but don't beat yourself up when you miss impossible goals. Be sure to celebrate the goals you do reach.

Maybe you haven't achieved the weight you

put on your driver's license, but you did lose five pounds this month. Don't dwell on the fact that you didn't meet that ideal weight. Instead, celebrate your five-pound weight loss. Maybe you didn't sell the most real estate in your office this month, but you did achieve a personal best. Celebrate your accomplishment!

God wants you to celebrate you and the good things you achieve. He doesn't expect you to be perfect all the time, so why should you expect that?

Ask God to help you feel happier with yourself and your accomplishments. Start celebrating the person that God made you to be. And always remember this: You may never be perfect, but you are perfectly loved by God.

Michelle Medlock Adams
Secrets of Happiness

Blessed Storms

*He got up and rebuked the wind and the raging
waters; the storm subsided, and all was calm.
"Where is your faith?" he asked his disciples.*

LUKE 8:24–25 NIV

*J*esus' disciples were fishermen—experienced
men of the sea—whose livelihood before they
followed Christ meant they were out in their boats
every day. Yet this storm was so fierce they were
afraid they were going to drown. The boat was
being swamped, filling with water from the height
and ferocity of the waves and the wind whipping
the water into their boat.

Jesus had the power to stop what no man could
ever dream of stopping—the force of nature.
They had forgotten that Jesus was the Creator. He
spoke the world into existence; it was nothing for

Him to calm the storm.

Jesus knew there would be a storm; He knew they would come out of it. He wanted the disciples to respond in faith. Peter later wrote that our faith would be tested—tried by various trials—to prove its genuineness and worth. Then it would become strong enough to praise, honor, and glorify the Lord.

Have you thought to embrace these trials that will inevitably come—our own perfect storms? To "greatly rejoice," as Peter tells us in 1 Peter, as we are "grieved" or distressed by these challenges that come our way. Peter learned that these difficulties in life—these tests of our faith—are good things, if we allow God to work through them and in us to bring Him praise, honor, and glory.

Missy Horsfall
Circle of Friends

Complete Devotion

The keeper of the prison did not look into anything that was under Joseph's authority, because the Lord was with him; and whatever he did, the Lord made it prosper.

GENESIS 39:23 NKJV

No matter where Joseph went, whatever he did prospered. Even when tossed in prison, he ended up running the place. You couldn't call this young son of Jacob a slacker. But how did he do it?

Doubtless Joseph was an intelligent young man and a hard worker, but that alone cannot account for his ability to make the most of any situation.

We, too, have some smarts and work hard yet we don't necessarily end up running our companies.

Joseph's difference lay in his complete devotion to God. Instead of bemoaning his awful lot in life, Joseph called on God for help, did what he was given to do, and did it exceptionally well. Facing desperate situations, he had thrown himself totally on his Lord, not his own mental abilities or skills. By doing that, he received God's blessings on all he did.

Today, learn from Joseph. Place all you have and are in God's hands, to use as He will. Even if you never become president, your blessings will surprise you.

Pamela McQuade
Daily Wisdom for the Workplace

Worthy Words

"If you repent, I will restore you that you may serve me; if you utter worthy, not worthless words, you will be my spokesman."

JEREMIAH 15:19 NIV

It seemed almost factual at the time, the quick assessment I'd made of my husband's actions. But it hurt. He just stared at me and I stared back, feeling justified at the moment after one of my words had slashed him to the bone. Then I saw his heart was bleeding.

How long had it been since I'd done that? So long, I'd imagined my nasty talent tamed, but here it was back again in fighting form. What had I done? *Oh, dear God, what a mess I've made. Can this wound I've caused be healed? Forgive me, Lord.*

Like many in Christian ministry, it's my strengths that trip me. Words, often too many of them, once marched freely off my tongue. Had God not reduced me to brokenness more than once over my unleashed humor, angry reactions, and careless comments? I'd surrendered my tongue to Him again and again. My apology to my husband came quickly, sincere to the core. He accepted.

But God woke me early in the morning with a warning from Jeremiah, the mournful prophet of unwelcome words. "If you repent, I will restore you that you may serve me; if you utter worthy, not worthless words, you will be my spokesman." Yes, Lord. I get Your message. There's no mixing my worthless words with Your life-giving ones. It's one or the other. I want Your words, Lord, today and every day.

Virelle Kidder

Blessed Fellowship

For where two or three are gathered together in my name, there am I in the midst of them.

MATTHEW 18:20 KJV

A few years ago my husband and I were in Ohio, where I was scheduled to do some book signings. We were pleased when some of our Amish friends from Pennsylvania hired a driver to bring them to Ohio so we could spend a few days together. Even though our time was short, the fellowship we had was sweet. We did some shopping, shared a few meals, and attended church together. We told stories from the past, talked about the future, and exchanged prayer requests. Even though our Amish friends dress differently than we do, and live a different lifestyle, we have become close and enjoy each other's company.

We consider this couple to be some of our dearest friends, and look forward to our times of fellowship with them.

God doesn't want us to close ourselves off from others. He wants us to spend time with other believers and gather in His name. I always feel the presence of God when I'm with a dear Christian friend. When we share our joys, sorrows, and prayer requests with others we feel comforted and not alone.

Do you know of someone who's lonely or needs a friend? Why not find some time to fellowship with that person this week? You'll both feel blessed if you do.

Wanda E. Brunstetter
A Celebration of the Simple Life

Knowing God

[For my determined purpose is] that I may know Him [that I may progressively become more deeply and intimately acquainted with Him, perceiving and recognizing and understanding the wonders of His Person more strongly and more clearly].

PHILIPPIANS 3:10 AMP

To know God as He really is in His essential nature and character is to have reached the absolute and unchangeable and utterly satisfying foundation upon which can be reared the whole superstructure of our religious life.

The poorer and more imperfect is one's conception of God, the more fervent and intense will be one's efforts to propitiate Him and to put Him into a good humor; whereas on the other hand, the higher and truer is the knowledge of the goodness and unselfishness of God, the less anxiety and fuss and wrestling and agonizing will there be in one's worship. A good and unselfish God will be sure to do right anyhow, whether we try to propitiate Him or not, and we can safely trust Him to carry on His affairs with very little advice from us.

In human relations we may know a great deal about a person without at all necessarily coming into any actual acquaintance with that person; and it is the same in our relations with God. We are so accustomed to think that knowing things about Him is sufficient—what He has done, what He has said, what His plans are, and what are the doctrines concerning Him—that we stop short of that knowledge of what He really is in nature and character, which is the only satisfactory knowledge.

Hannah Whitall Smith
The Unselfishness of God

No More Marching

Just as man is destined to die once, and after that to face judgment, so Christ was sacrificed once to take away the sins of many people; and he will appear a second time, not to bear sin, but to bring salvation to those who are waiting for him.

HEBREWS 9:27–28 NIV

Every year at Yom Kippur, my friend who lives in Israel takes off his sandals and puts on tennis shoes because leather is traditionally eschewed on high holy days for being too comfortable. He walks—because riding in an automobile or even riding a bicycle would be considered "working"— to a big temple in downtown Jerusalem. And there he tries to remember every single time he's broken the law of God in the past year. He earnestly believes that this arduous task is what God demands from him.

There is no joy in this exercise, no perfecting of his conscience, and no sense of completion, because this will not be the last time he marches to temple to recount his sin. He knows he'll have to repeat the whole process all over again next year if he has any hope of receiving God's justice, let alone mercy.

I couldn't do it. I can't remember all the times I sinned in the last week, much less in the last year. If my relationship with God depended on my memory or ritualistic repetition, I'd be in a lot of trouble. But it doesn't. There is a better road that leads to reconciliation with God. And Jesus died to pave it for us.

Lisa Harper
Holding Out for a Hero

Assurance of Blessings

I will bless you [with abundant increase of favors]...
and you will be a blessing [dispensing good to others].

GENESIS 12:2 AMP

The Bible is full of God's blessings for our lives, full of positive words, promises granted to those who choose to follow Him, who choose to believe in His assurances. We can be filled with assurance that wherever we go, God will bless us.

Is your faith strong enough and your mind open enough to make room for God's bounty of blessings? Perhaps you feel you are undeserving. If so, plant the words of Hebrews 11:6 in your heart: "Without faith it is impossible to please and be satisfactory to Him. For whoever would come near to God must [necessarily] believe that God exists and that He is the rewarder of those who

earnestly and diligently seek Him [out]" (AMP).
It's not a matter of deserving but of firm faith,
great expectation, and sincere seeking.

Drop your doubt and disbelief, let go of negative thinking, and make room in your arms to
receive God's blessings.

Thank God for eternal promises, past blessings,
and the assurance of blessings to come. By doing
so, you'll avoid the pitfall of seeing the world
through eyes of discouragement. Praise and thank
God for all His blessings, focusing on the Giver
and not on the gift.

Choose to believe that Christ loves you and is
blessing you even in the midst of trials. He always
goes before you, planting blessings on your path.

Donna K. Maltese
Power Prayers to Start Your Day

Knowing Our Place

"I'm not doing this for you.
Get this through your thick heads!"

EZEKIEL 36:32 MSG

I was visiting an elderly lady who was extremely hard of hearing. As we finished our conversation, I asked her if I could pray. She consented and I knelt down in front of her so she could hear me better. I bowed my head and offered up a heartfelt prayer.

As I said "Amen," I looked up and she said, "You are such a natural. . . ." My heart just melted and I thought, *Ahhh. Yes, this is where I am supposed to be. God is using me and has confirmed my being here.* And then she finished her sentence. "You are such a natural. . .blond, aren't you?" As I broke out in a chuckle, I realized she had been studying my scalp the entire time I was praying. She hadn't heard a word I said.

Humility is a great teacher! Have you ever caught yourself taking yourself a little too seriously? As I know that the God of the universe loves me with an everlasting love, has given me an identity in Christ that doesn't quit, calls me Chosen, Friend, and Beloved—I also know that He has shared these things with me for His glory.

We would be wise to remember that He alone has center stage.

Jocelyn Hamsher
Circle of Friends

The Bread of Life

O taste and see that the Lord is good:
blessed is the man that trusteth in him.

PSALM 34:8 KJV

A wonderful crusty loaf of bread tastes so good when you're hungry. Those "artisan loaves" of old-fashioned bread are my favorite. A breakfast piece of toast often fuels the start of my day.

Jesus called Himself "the bread of life" (John 6:35 KJV), and as I crunch into a favorite slice of bread, I can understand that He's talking on two levels. First, He provides the sustenance we all need. Without Him, we're spiritually empty. But I think today's verse on taste also applies to Jesus the bread of life. Not only does the bread of Jesus fuel the spiritual day, it tastes good. We're blessed when we trust Jesus, not only because He brings new life, but because He brings a delight to life that's missing from unbelievers' existence.

Living for Jesus isn't a matter of gritting your teeth and living in a cheerless way. Instead, faith in Him brings new joys into our lives—even better than the taste of a nice, crunchy loaf of bread.

Pamela McQuade
Daily Wisdom for the Workplace

Doing His Will

Therefore, I urge you, brothers, in view of God's mercy, to offer your bodies as living sacrifices, holy and pleasing to God—this is your spiritual act of worship.

ROMANS 12:1 NIV

Is it thought anything so very extraordinary and high-flown, when a bride deliberately prefers wearing a color which was not her own taste or choice, because her husband likes to see her in it?

Is it very unnatural that it is no distress to her to do what he asks her to do, or to go with him where he asks her to come, even without question or explanation, instead of doing what or going where she would undoubtedly have preferred if she did not know and love him?

Is it very surprising if this lasts beyond the

wedding day, and if year after year she still finds it her greatest pleasure to please him, quite irrespective of what used to be her own ways and likings?

Yet in this case she is not helped by any promise or power on his part to make her wish what he wishes. But He who so wonderfully condescends to call Himself the Bridegroom of His church, and who claims our fullest love and trust, has promised and has power to work in us to will. Shall we not claim His promise and rely on His mighty power, and say, not self-confidently, but looking only unto Jesus—"Keep my will, for it is Thine; it shall be no longer mine!"

Frances Ridley Havergal
Kept for the Master's Use

Giving Our Troubles to God

"Come to Me, all who are weary and heavy-laden, and I will give you rest."

MATTHEW 11:28 NASB

Behold, I am thy God, and I am with thee to
help thee.

In the darkness I will be to thee a light, and
when thou walkest alone, I will be thy companion.

Have I spoken, and will I not bring it to pass?

Have I promised and will I not perform it?

Yes, I will surely do all that I have said.

For My hand shall be upon thee.

When thou wakest and when thou sleepest,

I shall be ever at thy right hand,

   and I shall give thee strength.

      For thou art My child, and thy needs are
My constant care.

Therefore I have asked thee to roll thy burdens and thine anxieties upon Me,

for every circumstance which toucheth thee is My concern.

Yea, I am not only concerned,

but I am able to deliver thee and I will deliver thee as surely as thou shalt rest thy case in My hands.

Frances J. Roberts
Dialogues with God

Surrender

*We continue to shout our praise even when we're
hemmed in with troubles, because we know how
troubles can develop passionate patience in us, and
how that patience in turn forges the tempered steel of
virtue, keeping us alert for whatever God will do next.*

Romans 5:3–4 MSG

I have never met anyone who said, "Relinquishment is easy." For most of us, making the choice to
release our control over our spouse, child, friend,
job, or longed-for dream feels like someone is
prying our fingers open one by one and expos-
ing our defenseless hearts. Sometimes, when we
have loss upon loss, we think we deserve to be in
control of certain outcomes, if only to protect
ourselves from additional hurt and pain. It seems
the most irrational thing we can do is to let go one

more time. We battle with conflicting emotions and "duke it out with God," sometimes through prayer, but occasionally by being obstinate. Our honest thoughts reveal our deep fears. So many bad things have happened to me. How much more will God require? It seems irrational and unreasonable to lay what is precious to me on the altar again. Letting go of our grip on predictable results and trusting God with our heart offering is one of the most challenging choices we make.

Carol Kent
A New Kind of Normal

Blessed Refreshment

*Come to Me, all you who labor and are heavy-laden
and overburdened, and I will cause you to rest.
[I will ease and relieve and refresh your souls.]*

MATTHEW 11:28 AMP

Some days we are pulled every which way. At
times even our home may be a source of tension.
During such adversity our true colors tend to
show, revealing who we are and where we are putting our trust.

Stress is not a new problem. Remember Elijah?
After an amazing victory on Mount Carmel,
we find this prophet running for his life as fear
replaced faith. First Kings 19 tells us that once he
made his escape, Elijah rested beneath a broom
tree where he "prayed that he might die. 'I have
had enough, LORD,' he said. 'Take my life'" (verse

4 NIV). Then he lay down and fell asleep.

Have you ever felt like Elijah, saying, "Lord, I can't take it anymore," and then fallen into bed? But fortunately, God is ready to minster to us in the midst of stress.

But where to find a broom tree? Perhaps it would be easier for us to find a broom closet, a quiet place of prayer, and there seek out Jesus Christ. He alone is the One who can get us through the storms of life.

Continually turn to God, resting in his presence, trusting in Him, and allowing Him to carry your load. Build your life not on the world and its pleasures but on His words, hearing them and putting them into practice, and your foundation will be able to resist the cracks brought on by the storms of life.

Donna K. Maltese
Power Prayers to Start Your Day

The Blessings of Change

By faith Abraham, when called to go to a place he would later receive as his inheritance, obeyed and went, even though he did not know where he was going.

HEBREWS 11:8 NIV

As we look down the Hall of Biblical Fame in search of inspiring characters who were blessed above measure, one thing rings true: These people opened their hands to God. People like Abraham. Truly Abraham was open. He had to be. He had no idea where he was going! But God knew.

I will be the first to admit it: I hate change— hate it, hate it, hate it! And doesn't it seem the moment you settle into a groove and get comfortable, God comes along and says, "Okay, it's time to pull up the stakes and move on"?

"But wait a minute, God!" you

say. "I was just getting comfortable." God knows that comfortable is a dangerous place. The more comfortable we become, the less dependent on God we become. And so He shakes up the mix of our lives and keeps us moving. When we arrive at the destination He selected, we rejoice. "Gee, Lord!" we exclaim, "You should have told me—I would have done this sooner."

Well, that's exactly why He didn't. You would have moved ahead of His plan and missed it. God wants us to be open to His voice and His leading every step of the way. He will always lead us down the right path.

Michelle McKinney Hammond
How to Be Blessed and Highly Favored

Because You're You

"The LORD your God is with you, he is mighty to save.
He will take great delight in you, he will quiet you with
His love, he will rejoice over you with singing."

ZEPHANIAH 3:17 NIV

Growing up, I used to ask my brother why he didn't like me, and he told me, "Because you're you." That's often the message we get from the world, isn't it? That you're not good enough, pretty enough, skinny enough, talented enough, smart enough, worthy enough. You are just not enough.

But we so desperately look for love and approval. It may be from siblings, parents, boyfriends, husbands, friends, or wherever we can get it. Often feeling like we have to earn it—we have to be something or do something worthy of it. But the truth is we don't have to look very far—that love is there all along for us, and that it exceeds any earthly love we could find.

Your Father takes great delight in you. He rejoices over you. You are His creation, His child, and there is nothing you can do to change that! You can't earn His love, and you can't lose it. He loves you because He is God and because He is good. He loves you simply because you're you.

Emily Smith
Circle of Friends

"Hopelessly Devoted"

Near the cross of Jesus stood his mother, his mother's sister, Mary the wife of Clopas, and Mary Magdalene.

JOHN 19:25 NIV

I grew up watching *Grease*, starring John Travolta and Olivia Newton-John. I love it when she walks around in her nightgown, singing "Hopelessly Devoted to You." Of course, in that scene, she is singing of her character's devotion to Travolta's character—her summer love.

Devotion can be a very noble character trait. You see glimpses of devotion throughout the Bible—especially in the story of the Cross. Jesus was devoted to the Father—so much so that He was willing to die a horrible death to fulfill God's salvation plan so that we could spend eternity with Him. And though some of Jesus' followers dissociated themselves from Jesus for fear of being crucified, too, the women didn't disown Him. It tells us in John 19:25 that Mary, the mother of Jesus; Jesus' aunt; Mary the wife of Clopas; and Mary Magdalene stayed at the foot of the Cross, even though they were implicating themselves by being there.

That is the kind of devotion that makes a difference. What are you truly devoted to? Are you willing to spend time at the foot of the Cross, just basking in His presence? That's devotion. The Word says if you seek Him, all of the other things will be added to you.

Michelle Medlock Adams
Secrets of Beauty

Choose Life

Whatever is true, whatever is noble, whatever is right, whatever is pure, whatever is lovely, whatever is admirable—if anything is excellent or praiseworthy—think about such things.

PHILIPPIANS 4:8 NIV

There is a lot of talk about positive thinking. Some of it is helpful and some of it is deceitful. Take for instance the phrase, "You can be anything you want to be in life." This is not true. We each have our own unique set of skills and weaknesses.

In Deuteronomy chapter 30, the children of Israel were about to enter the promised land. They had a big job to do. The land was occupied and the armies of Israel had to defeat its inhabitants and take over the land.

God told them in verses 19 and 20 (NIV), "I have set before you life and death, blessings and curses. Now choose life, so that you and your children may live and that you may love the LORD your God, listen to his voice, and hold fast to him. For the LORD is your life, and he will give you many years in the land he swore to give to your fathers, Abraham, Isaac and Jacob."

In this world we always have life and death, blessings and curses before us. And we can choose what to focus on. It's more than seeing the glass half full, it's seeing God's goodness and love in our lives. It's also choosing who we are going to be, and deciding to be a blessing.

Julie Hufstetler
Singer, Songwriter

Hearing His Voice

"I am the good shepherd. . . . My sheep listen to my voice; I know them, and they follow me."

JOHN 10:14, 27 NIV

Does God still speak to us today? I'm absolutely sure He does. But don't take my word for it—take Jesus' word. . . .

Since God continues to speak today, why do we have such difficulty recognizing His voice? Why don't we hear Him more often? Hearing God's voice should be part of the normal, everyday experience for a child of God. It is God's silence that should give us reason for concern, for in times past, God's silence was a form of punishment for disobedience. Also, hearing God's voice is not only for the "super Christian," if there is such a thing. It is for the uneducated fisherman, the woman in the kitchen, the leprous outcast, the tax collector in a tree, and for you and me. . . .

I haven't heard God's audible voice, but He does speak to me on a regular basis. I've felt His nudge in the kitchen as I've mopped the linoleum floor; I've recognized His tug as I've pulled off the highway in an overheated car; I've sensed His peaceful wooing as I've struggled to weather tumultuous storms; I've heard echoes of His laughter as He's instructed me to learn from the children in my care; I've sensed His presence as I spent time meditating on the scriptures.

My hope and prayer is that you will begin to recognize God's presence in your own life and become a woman who listens to God.

Sharon Jaynes
Becoming a Woman Who Listens to God

The Love of Christ

For the love of Christ controls us, because we have concluded this: that one has died for all, therefore all have died; and he died for all, that those who live might no longer live for themselves but for him who for their sake died and was raised.

2 Corinthians 5:14–15 esv

What proportion of your moments do you think enough for Jesus? How many for the spirit of praise, and how many for the spirit of heaviness? Be explicit about it, and come to an understanding. If He is not to have all, then how much? Calculate, balance, and apportion. You will not be able to do this in heaven—you know it will be all praise there; but you are free to halve your service of praise here, or to make the proportion what you will.

Yet—He made you for His glory.

Yet—He chose you that you should be to the praise of His glory.

Yet—He loves you every moment, waters you every moment, watches you unslumberingly, cares for you unceasingly.

Yet—He died for you!

Dear friends, one can hardly write it without tears. Shall you or I remember all this love, and hesitate to give all our moments up to Him? Let us entrust Him with them, and ask Him to keep them all, every single one, for His own beloved self, and fill them all with His praise, and let them all be to His praise!

Frances Ridley Havergal
Kept for the Master's Use

He's Waiting to Listen

The earnest prayer of a righteous person has great
power and produces wonderful results.

James 5:16 nlt

It is easy to find excuses not to pray. We are too
busy, don't have time, don't know how, don't feel
like it, etc. But if we find ourselves too busy to do
what we have been told to do, then it stands to
reason we are doing some things that we were not
told to do. And if I pray without ceasing my work,
then I don't have an excuse. The best way to learn
to pray is to pray.

I have discovered that I will seldom pray if
I always wait until I feel like it. When I feel
the least like praying is when I find I need
prayer the most. Many only pray when
things go wrong, when there is

a crisis or disturbance in their lives. They use prayer as a last resort. While I am sure that God hears these prayers also, prayer is not something we do just because we are desperate. It is something we do because we want to communicate with the One who loves us. It is something He has asked us to do in order for us to develop a relationship with Him.

He longs for our communication with Him.

Gigi Graham Tchividjian
A Quiet Knowing

Time with God

There is a time for everything, and a season for every activity under heaven. . .a time to embrace and a time to refrain. . .a time to be silent and a time to speak.

ECCLESIASTES 3:1, 5, 7 NIV

About ten years ago, a friend set me up on a blind date with an enthusiastic gentleman whom we'll call "Bob." Following that date, Bob was relentless in his pursuit of me. He sent flowers, wrote letters, and sang songs on my answering machine to communicate his affection. Although my response to his overtures wasn't always positive, he was determined to win my affection.

Shakespeare would've been proud—Bob pitched some serious woo.

Of course, my old beau's passion pales significantly next to that of the Lover of our souls. God's perfect countenance splits into a grin, like a young bridegroom (see Isaiah 62:5) when He sees us coming. We should rejoice with wonder at being romanced by the Lord of the universe.

However, I've discovered I'm not very good at being wooed. I have a hard time enjoying God's gifts, savoring the sweetness of His letters, and paying attention while His love songs wash over my soul. I'm performance oriented, and my personality leans toward having way too many irons in the proverbial fire. I've only recently begun to practice the discipline of resting so that my heart will be pliant for His pursuit. I'm also learning that there are seasons when I desperately need to stop doing and simply collapse in His embrace.

Lisa Harper
What the Bible Is All About for Women

Open Doors

*"I know all the things you do, and I have opened a door
for you that no one can close. You have little strength,
yet you obeyed my word and did not deny me."*

REVELATION 3:8 NLT

God can open those stuck doors in our lives if we seek to obey and not deny Him.

"But that's hard work!" you may admit. Yes, standing firm for Jesus can be difficult. But when it is, perhaps it's because we've shut some doors on Him: the doors in our hearts that hide dark, sinful spaces. Jesus will not respond to our sin by forcing our doors open or running for skeleton keys. If we shut Him out, He lets us. Yet we'll hear His sweet, gentle voice right through that door. No matter how we try to avoid it, His Spirit calls to our souls.

When, in our feeble strength, instead of trying to clean out sin ourselves, we offer Him the keys to the portals we can't even begin to budge, His Spirit opens our nasty closets, empties them, and fills them to overflowing with love, joy, and peace. Suddenly, new doors fling wide before us, doors of Christian service and freedom from sin.

No one can shut a door Jesus opens. So today, offer Him the keys to your life's closed doors. Then walk through the doors He'll open for you.

Pamela McQuade
Daily Wisdom for the Workplace

Blessed Contentment

Faith is the confidence that what we hope for will actually happen; it gives us assurance about things we cannot see.

HEBREWS 11:1 NLT

Nothing but God can satisfy this loneliness of humanity. No change of circumstances, not even the dearest earthly ties could really satisfy the hungry depth of your soul for any length of time.

The question is how to bring one's self to be satisfied in God when there is no feeling. And I do not know what else to say but that it must be by faith. I confess it does seem an odd sort of thing to do, to become satisfied by saying one is satisfied when one is not. But is it not just what faith is described to be calling "those things which be not as though they were"

(Romans 4:17 KJV)?

And what else can we do? In my own case I just determined I would be satisfied with God alone. I gave up seeking after my feeling of satisfaction and consented to go through all the rest of my life with no feeling whatever, if this should be God's will. I said, "Lord, You are enough for me, just Yourself, without any of Your gifts or Your blessings. I have You, and I will be content. I choose to be content. I am content." I said this by faith. I still have to say it by faith often. It makes no difference how I feel. He is just the same, and He is with me, and I am His, and I am satisfied.

Hannah Whitall Smith
The Christian's Secret of a Happy Life

Blessed Gratitude

This is the message which we have heard from Him
and declare to you, that God is light
and in Him is no darkness at all.

1 JOHN 1:5 NKJV

As a scared little seven-year-old girl, I would sit in a narrow, dark, musty closet for hours at a time. But in those long, frightening hours, when my downright mean grandmother confined me to "keep me out of her way," I still had Jesus. I'd sing the hymns I'd learned at church, and when I didn't know the words, I'd make them up and just keep going: "Jesus loves me, this I know, for the Bible tells me so. Little ones to Him belong; they are weak but He is strong."

Today I speak to thousands of women who are locked in the closet of their own pain. I know women struggle every day with some hurt or another. I know because I've been there.

Like a mama longs to comfort her children, I want to embrace them with words of His comfort and love.

But sometimes, girlfriends, real love has to be tough.

And this is how it is: If you don't have the life you dreamed of, honey, you'd better learn to love the life you've got.

It all starts with an attitude of gratitude.

Even when life is not what we hoped it would be, we can concentrate on the good things and what we can do.

Thelma Wells
Kisses of Sunshine for Women

Title Index

Contributors

Michelle Medlock Adams has a diverse résumé featuring inspirational books, children's picture books, and greeting cards. Her insights have appeared in periodicals across America, including *Today's Christian Woman* and *Guideposts for Kids*. She lives in Fort Worth, Texas, with her husband, two daughters, and a "mini petting zoo."

Corrie ten Boom (1892–1983) was simply an ordinary, middle-aged Dutch spinster when the second world war began. By the time the conflict ended, she was literally transformed by the faith she had merely accepted and on a mission from God. By God's grace, Corrie survived the concentration camp and became a "tramp for the Lord," sharing in more than sixty nations the thrilling message that nothing, not even death, can separate us from God's love.

Jill Briscoe is the author of more than forty books—including devotionals, study guides, poetry, and children's books. She serves as Executive Editor of *Just Between Us* magazine and served on the board of World Relief and Christianity Today for more than twenty years. Jill and her husband make their home in Milwaukee, Wisconsin.

Award-winning, bestselling author, *Wanda E. Brunstetter* became fascinated with the Amish way of life when she first visited her husband's Mennonite relatives living in Pennsylvania. Wanda and her husband, Richard, live in Washington State but take every opportunity to visit Amish settlements throughout the States, where they have several Amish friends.

Amy Carmichael (1867–1951) was a Protestant Christian missionary in India, who opened an orphanage and founded a mission in Dohnavur. She served in India for fifty-six years without furlough and authored many books about her missionary work.

Patsy Clairmont is a speaker with Women of Faith Conferences and bestselling author of a number of books including *God Uses Cracked Pots* and *Normal Is Just a Setting on the Dryer*. In her speaking career she has blessed over four million women with her humor, vitality, and scriptural knowledge.

Fanny Crosby (1820-1915), blinded at infancy, became one of the most popular and prolific of all hymn writers. She wrote more than eight thousand hymns in her lifetime, including the best known

"Blessed Assurance," "Jesus Is Tenderly Calling You Home," "Praise Him, Praise Him," and "To God Be the Glory."

Elisabeth Elliot is a bestselling author of more than twenty books including *Passion and Purity*, *Be Still My Soul*, *The Path of Loneliness*, and *Keep a Quiet Heart*. She and her husband, Lars Gren, make their home in Magnolia, Massachusetts.

Carol L. Fitzpatrick is a bestselling author of nine books that have totaled nearly three quarters of a million books sold. She is a frequent conference speaker for writing groups and church groups. Carol and her husband have three grown children and three grandchildren. Although she credits her Midwest upbringing for instilling her core values, she has lived in California for nearly four decades.

Mabel Hale lived in Wichita, Kansas, in the early twentieth century. *Beautiful Girlhood* was her most popular book.

Michelle McKinney Hammond is a bestselling author, speaker, singer, and television co-host. She has authored more than thirty books including bestselling titles *The Diva Principle, Sassy, Single and Satisfied, 101 Ways to Get and Keep His Attention*, and *Secrets of an Irresistible Woman*. She makes her home in Chicago.

Jocelyn Hamsher is a gifted Bible Study teacher, writer, board member and speaker for Circle of Friends Ministries, and author of *Meet me at the Well*, a Bible study companion to Virelle Kidder's book by the same title. She lives in Sugarcreek, Ohio, with her husband Bruce and their three sons. She enjoys spending time with family, studying the Word of God, drinking coffee, and laughing with her husband.

Lisa Harper is an excellent communicator, author, speaker, and Bible teacher. She has spoken at Women of Faith, Moody Bible, Winsome Women, and Focus on the Family conferences and has written a number of books including *A Perfect Mess: How God Adores and Transforms Imperfect People Like Us*.

Frances Ridley Havergal (1836 –1879) was an English poet and hymn writer. "Take My Life and Let It Be" is one of her best known hymns. She also wrote hymn melodies, religious tracts, and works for children.

Missy Horsfall is a published magazine and greeting card writer and co-author of the novel *Double Honor*. A pastor's wife, she is a speaker and Bible study teacher for Circle of Friends and serves on the board overseeing their writing ministries. Missy also produces and co-hosts the COF radio program.

Julie Hufstetler is a singer/songwriter and worship leader who encourages and connects with listeners, whether she's singing alongside alongside recording artist Mark Schultz or with noted speakers like Sheila Walsh, Dee Brestin, and Nancy Leigh DeMoss. She and her husband, Guy, live in northeast Ohio with their three sons.

Sharon Jaynes is the author of thirteen books with Harvest House Publishers, Focus on the Family, and Moody Publishers and a frequent guest on national radio and television. She has also written numerous magazine articles and devotions for publications such as *Focus on the Family*, *Decision*, Crosswalk.com, and *In Touch*.

Barbara Johnson (1927–2007) was an award winning author and Women of Faith Speaker Emeritus with more than four million books in print and translated into ten foreign languages. She faced her long battle with cancer with the same humor and wisdom she met the many adversities of her life.

Jackie M. Johnson is an accomplished freelance writer and marketing copywriter. The author of *Power Prayers for Women*, she is a devoted prayer warrior and lives in Colorado.

Carol Kent is an internationally known speaker and author. Her books include, *When I Lay My Isaac Down*, *Becoming a Woman of Influence*, and *Mothers Have Angel Wing*s. She is president of Speak Up Speaker Services and the founder and director of Speak Up with Confidence seminars.

Virelle Kidder is a full-time writer and conference speaker and author of six books including *Meet Me at the Well* and *The Best Life Ain't Easy*. She is published in national magazines such as *Moody Magazine*, *Focus on the Family's Pastor's Family*, *Decision, Pray!, Journey, HomeLife*, and *Tapestry*.

Donna K. Maltese is a freelance writer, editor, and proofreader; publicist for a local Mennonite project; and the assistant director of RevWriter Writers Conferences.

Donna resides in Bucks County, Pennsylvania, with her husband and two children. She is a pastor's prayer partner and is active in her local church.

Pamela L. McQuade is a freelance writer and editor in Nutley, New Jersey, who has worked with numerous publishers. Her Barbour credits include *The Word on Life*, *Daily Wisdom for Couples*, and *Prayers and Promises*, all coauthored with Toni Sortor. Pam and her husband share their home with basset hounds and are involved in basset hound rescue.

Beth Moore, one of the best known Bible teachers in the evangelical Christian marketplace, has written numerous books and Bible studies. She is a wife and mother of two grown daughters and lives in Houston, Texas, where she leads Living Proof Ministries and teaches an adult Sunday school class at her church.

Stormie Omartian is a popular writer, speaker, and author. She is the author of the bestselling The Power of a Praying® books as well as many other titles. She and her husband have been married for thirty years and have three grown children.

Donna Partow is an author and motivational speaker. Her books, including *This Isn't the Life I Signed Up For. . .but I'm Finding Hope and Healing* and *Becoming a Vessel God Can Use*, have sold almost a million copies and her ministry Pieces4Peace reaches into the largest Muslim city in the world.

Ramona Richards is a freelance writer and editor living in Tennessee. Formerly the editor of *Ideals* magazine, Ramona has also edited children's books, fiction, nonfiction, study Bibles, and reference books for major Christian publishers. She is the author of *A Moment with God for Single Parents*.

Frances J. Roberts (1918–2009) is best known for her classic devotional *Come Away My Beloved*. She founded The King's Press in 1964, where she authored and published *Come Away* and eight other books, selling over 1.5 million copies in the last thirty years.

Emily Smith lives in Greenfield, Indiana, with her wonderful husband Eric. Married for two years, the only children they currently have are four-legged. Emily works for a home health agency and is a weekly blogger for the Circle of Friends Web site. She loves reading, cooking, and spending time with family.

Hannah Whitall Smith (1832–1911) was born into a strict Quaker home in Philadelphia and became a major influence in the Holiness movement of the late nineteenth century. Besides *The Christian's Secret of a Happy Life*, Smith also wrote *The God of All Comfort* and an autobiography, *The Unselfishness of God*.

Gigi Graham Tchividjian, daughter of Billy and Ruth Graham, is a busy wife, mother, grandmother, author, and speaker. She currently writes a regular column for *Christian Parenting* magazine and has written four books, including *Weather of the Heart* and *A Search for Serenity*.

Lysa TerKeurst is a nationally known speaker and president of the Proverbs 31 Ministry. An award winning author of twelve books including *Becoming More Than a Good Bible Study Girl*, she has been featured on Focus on the Family, Family Life Today, Good Morning America, and in *Woman's Day* magazine.

Lisa Troyer, co-founder and president of Circle of Friends Ministries, is a singer/songwriter, radio host, worship leader, and speaker. Her releases include *Pour Your Love Down* (with the COF Worship Team), *Forever*, and her latest worship CD, *Meet Me at the Well*, companion to the book by Virelle Kidder.

Sheila Walsh is a unique combination of international author, speaker, worship leader, television talk show host, and Bible teacher. She is a speaker with Women of Faith and bestselling author of her memoir *Honestly* and the Gold Medallion Award nominee *The Heartache No One Sees*.

Elizabeth Ward lives in Elida, Ohio, with her husband and three boys. A homeschooling mom, Bible teacher, and mentor, Elizabeth is also co-director of the Elida Teens for Christ high school chapter, a volunteer Bible teacher at a juvenile detention center, and is currently a host for Children's Medical Missions.

Thelma Wells, an international speaker including Women of Faith conferences, founded The Daughters of Zion Leadership Mentoring Program as well as Women of God Ministries. She is author of numerous books including *Listen Up, Honey, Good News for Your Soul* and *Don't Give In...God Wants You to Win.*

Permissions

Scripture
Index

What Is Circle of Friends?

Circle of Friends Ministries, Inc. is a nonprofit organization established to build a pathway for women to come into a personal relationship with Jesus Christ and to build Christian unity among women. Our mission is to honor Jesus Christ through meeting the needs of women in our local, national, and international communities. Our vision is to be women who are committed to Jesus Christ, obediently seeking God's will and fulfilling our life mission as Christ-followers. As individuals and as a corporate group, we minister a Christ-centered hope, biblically-based encouragement, and unconditional love by offering God-honoring, Word-based teaching, worship, accountability, and fellowship to women in a nondenominational environment through speaker services, worship teams, daily web blogs and devotionals, radio programs, and GirlFriends teen events.

COF also partners with churches and women's groups to bring conferences, retreats, Bible studies, concerts, simulcasts, and servant evangelism projects to their communities. We have a Marketplace Ministry teaching kingdom principles in the workplace and are committed to undergird, with prayer and financial support, foreign mission projects that impact the world for Jesus Christ. Our goal is to evangelize the lost and edify the Body of Christ, by touching the lives of women—locally, nationally, and globally.